"TINY CHILDREN ARE NOT HORSES..."

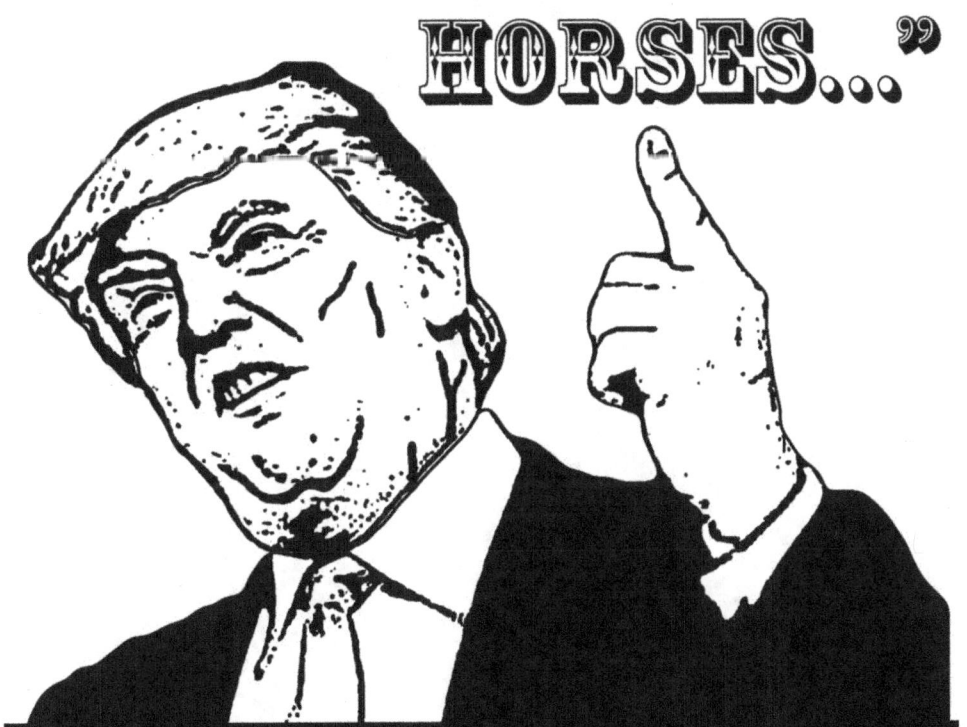

THE
TRUMP
COLORING BOOK

Pictures and Quotes from our
Great President, *the Stable Genius*

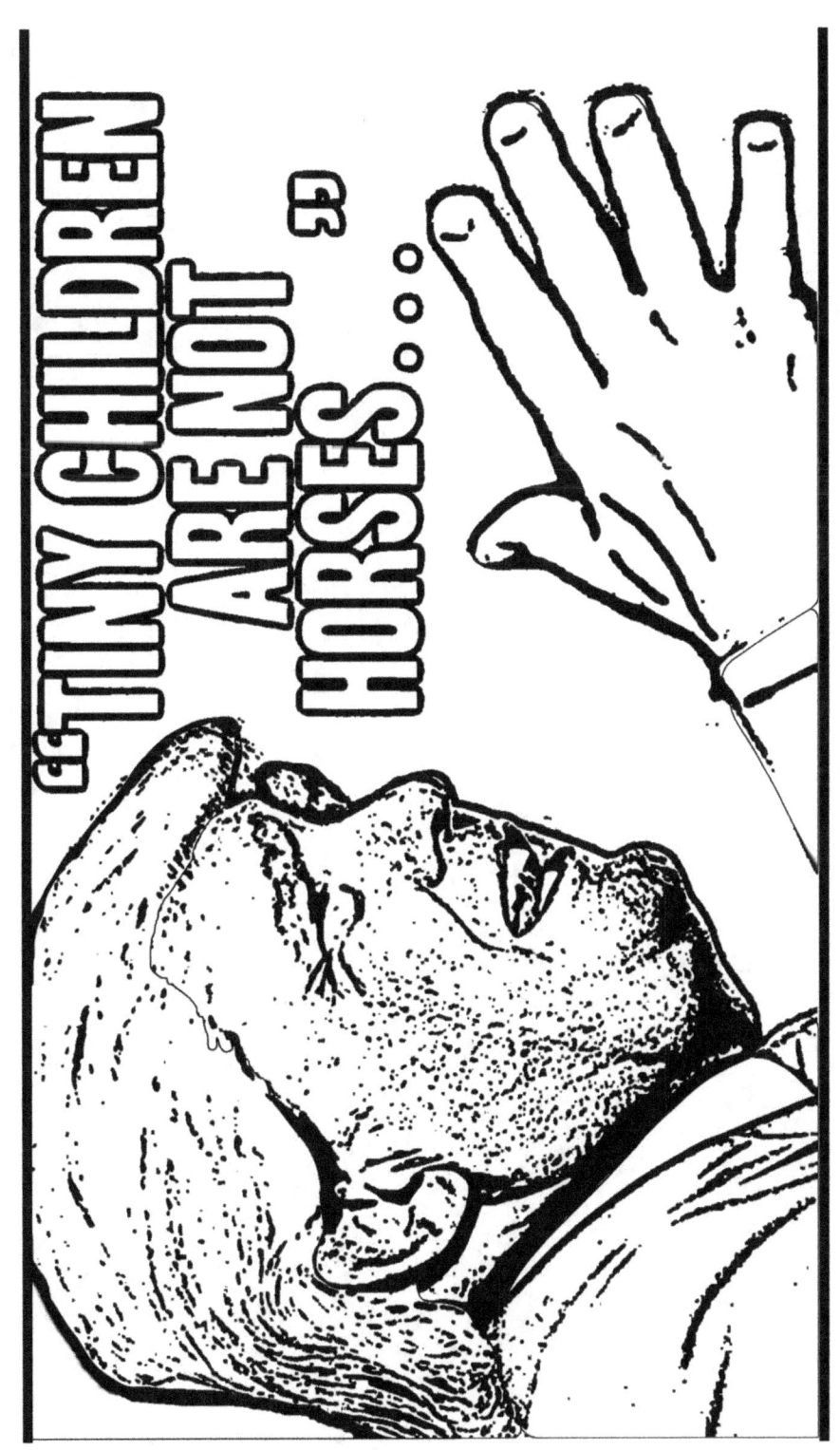

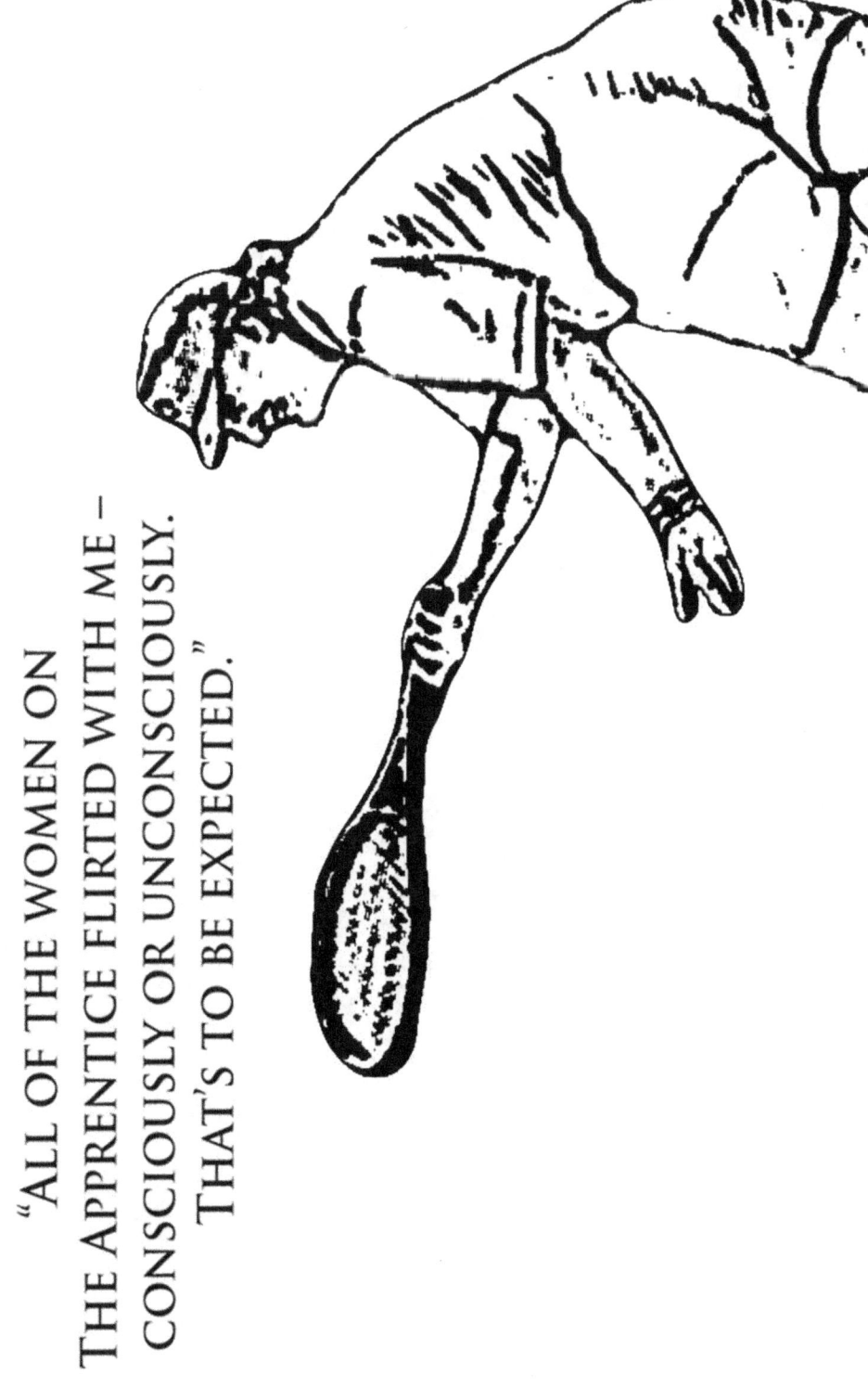

"ALL OF THE WOMEN ON
THE APPRENTICE FLIRTED WITH ME –
CONSCIOUSLY OR UNCONSCIOUSLY.
THAT'S TO BE EXPECTED."

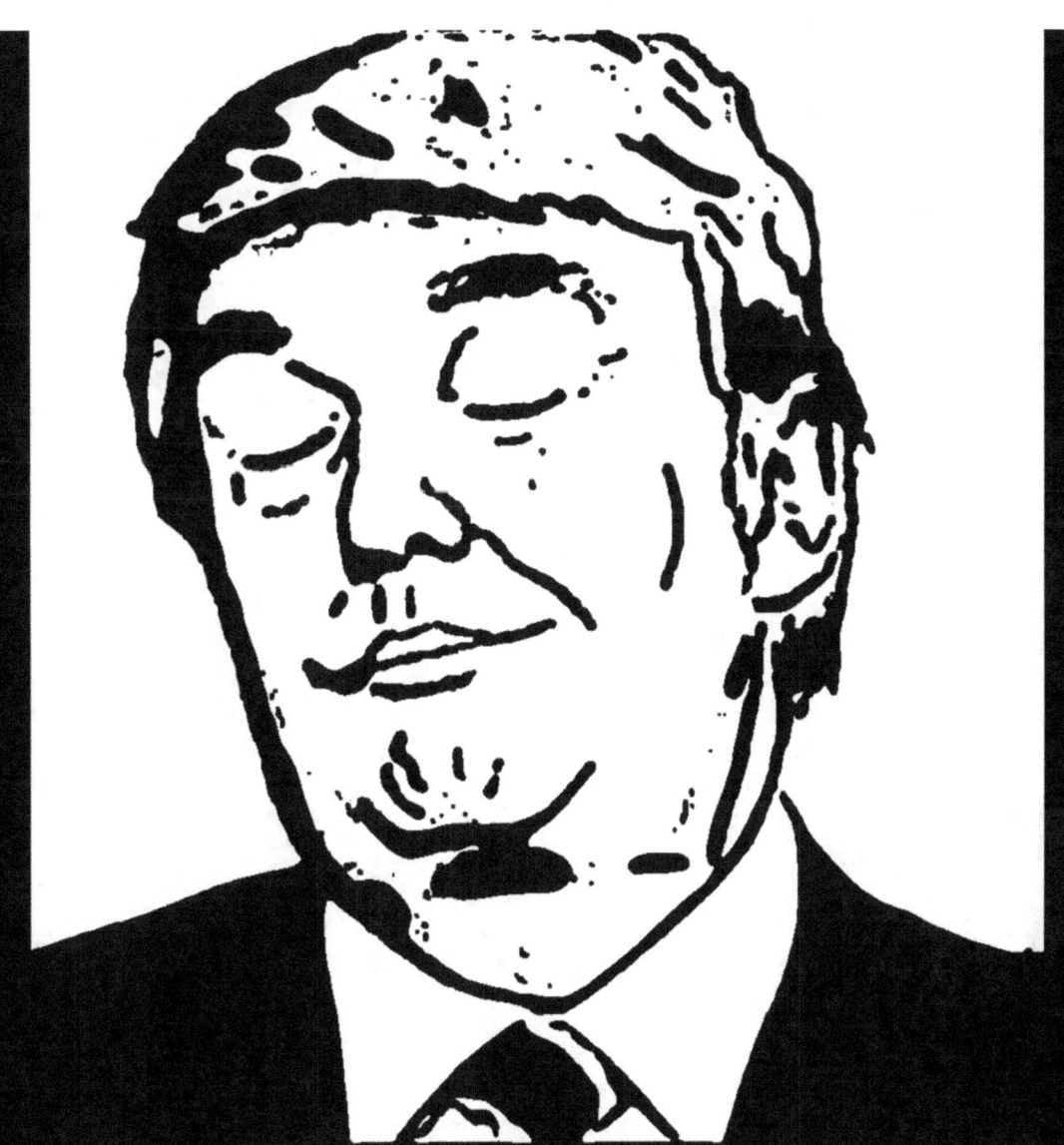

"THE BEAUTY OF ME IS THAT I'M VERY RICH."

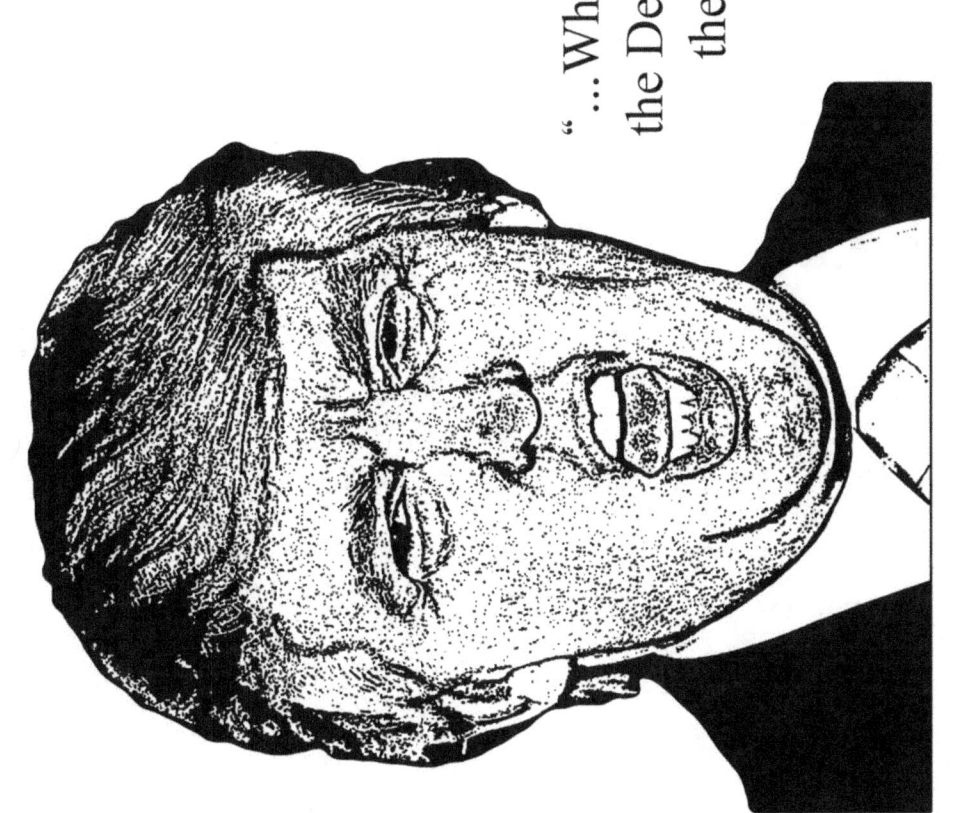

"... Why aren't Crooked Hillary & the Dems the focus???? ... Also, there is NO COLLUSION!"

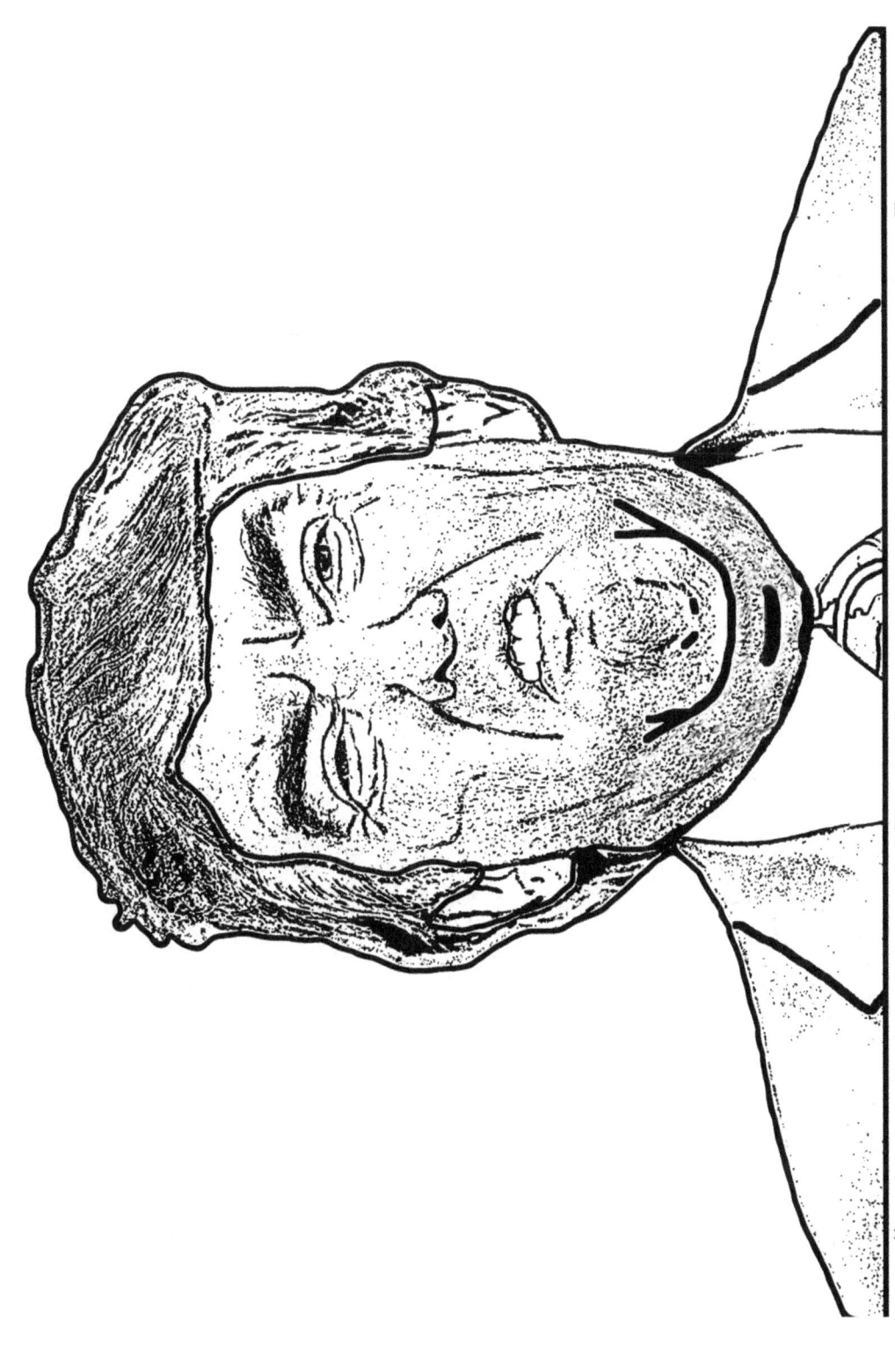

"MY TWITTER HAS BECOME SO POWERFUL THAT I CAN ACTUALLY MAKE MY ENEMIES TELL THE TRUTH."

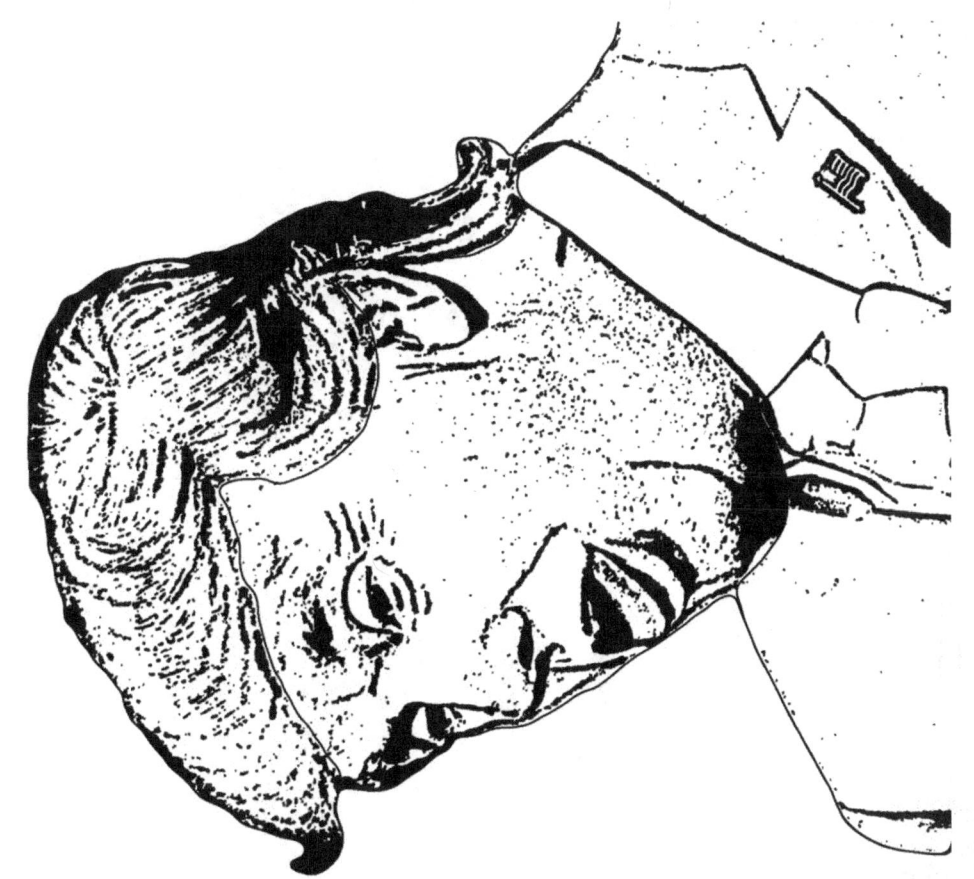

"If I were running 'The View', I'd fire Rosie O'Donnell. I mean, I'd look at her right in that fat, ugly face of hers, I'd say 'Rosie, you're fired.'"

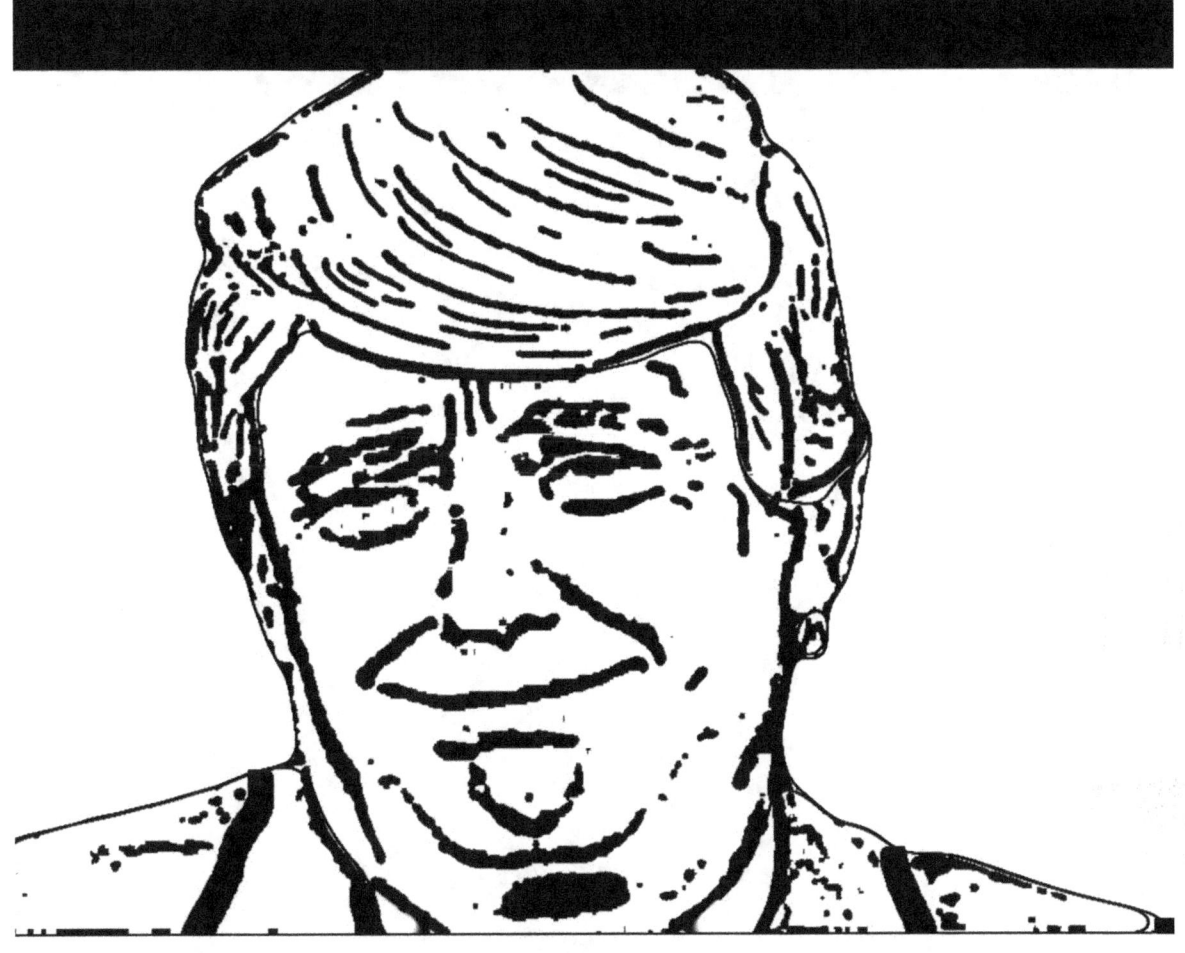

"One of they key problems today is that politics is such a disgrace. Good people don't go into government."

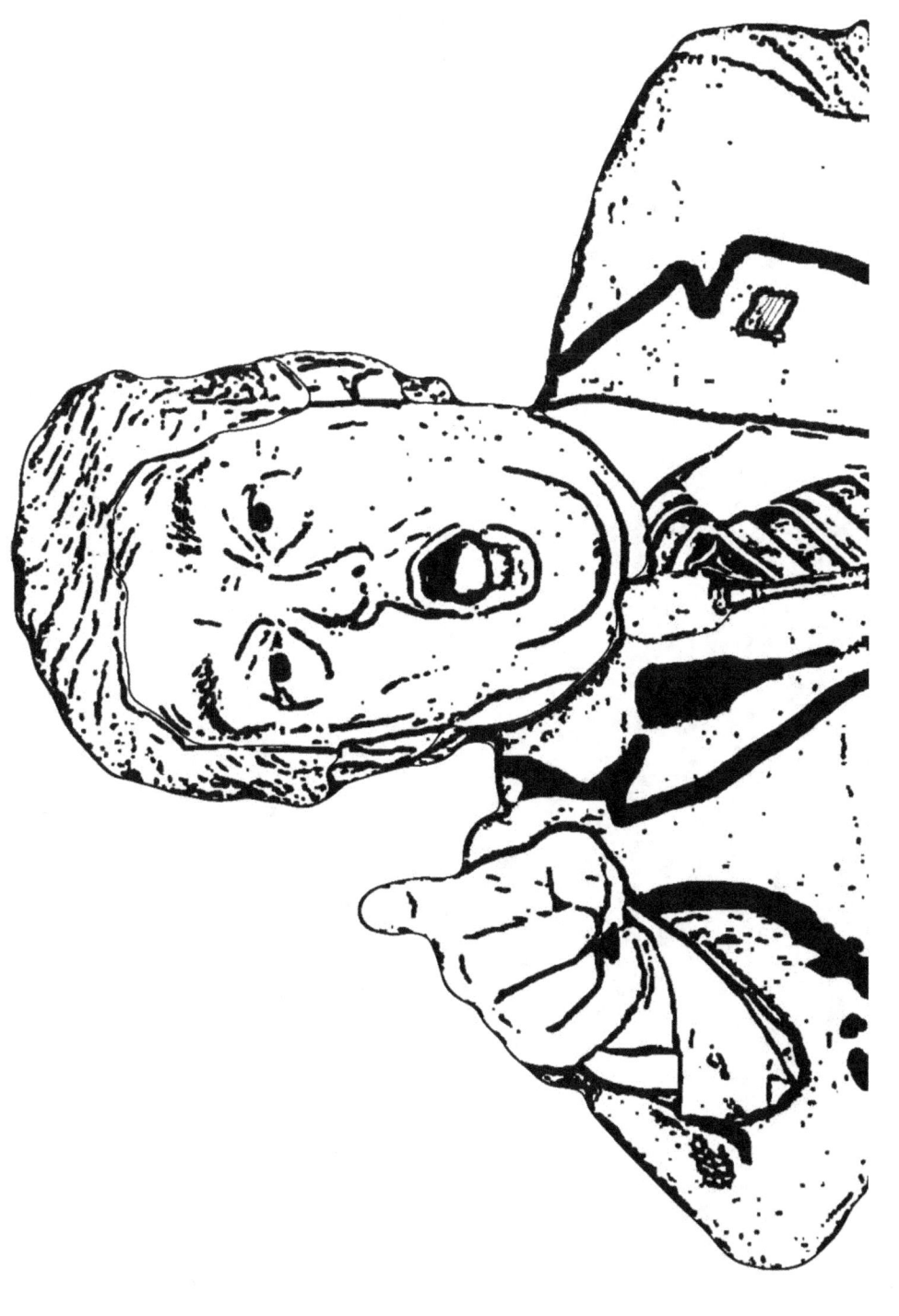

"LYIN' TED CRUZ JUST USED A PICTURE OF MELANIA FROM A SHOOT IN HIS AD. BE CAREFUL, LYIN' TED, OR I WILL SPILL THE BEANS ON YOUR WIFE!"

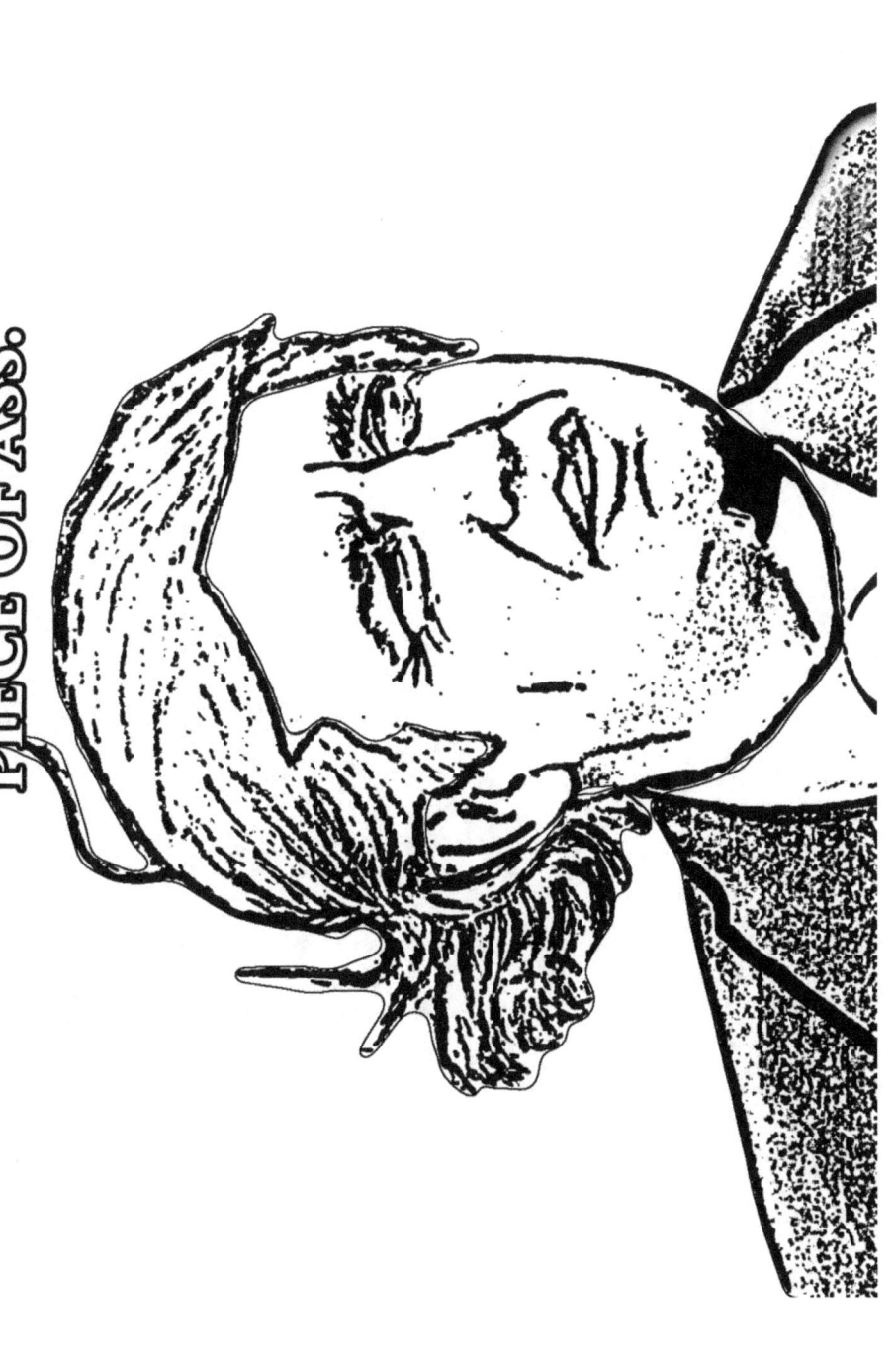

"YOU KNOW, IT REALLY DOESN'T MATTER WHAT THE MEDIA WRITE AS LONG AS YOU'VE GOT A YOUNG, AND BEAUTIFUL, PIECE OF ASS."

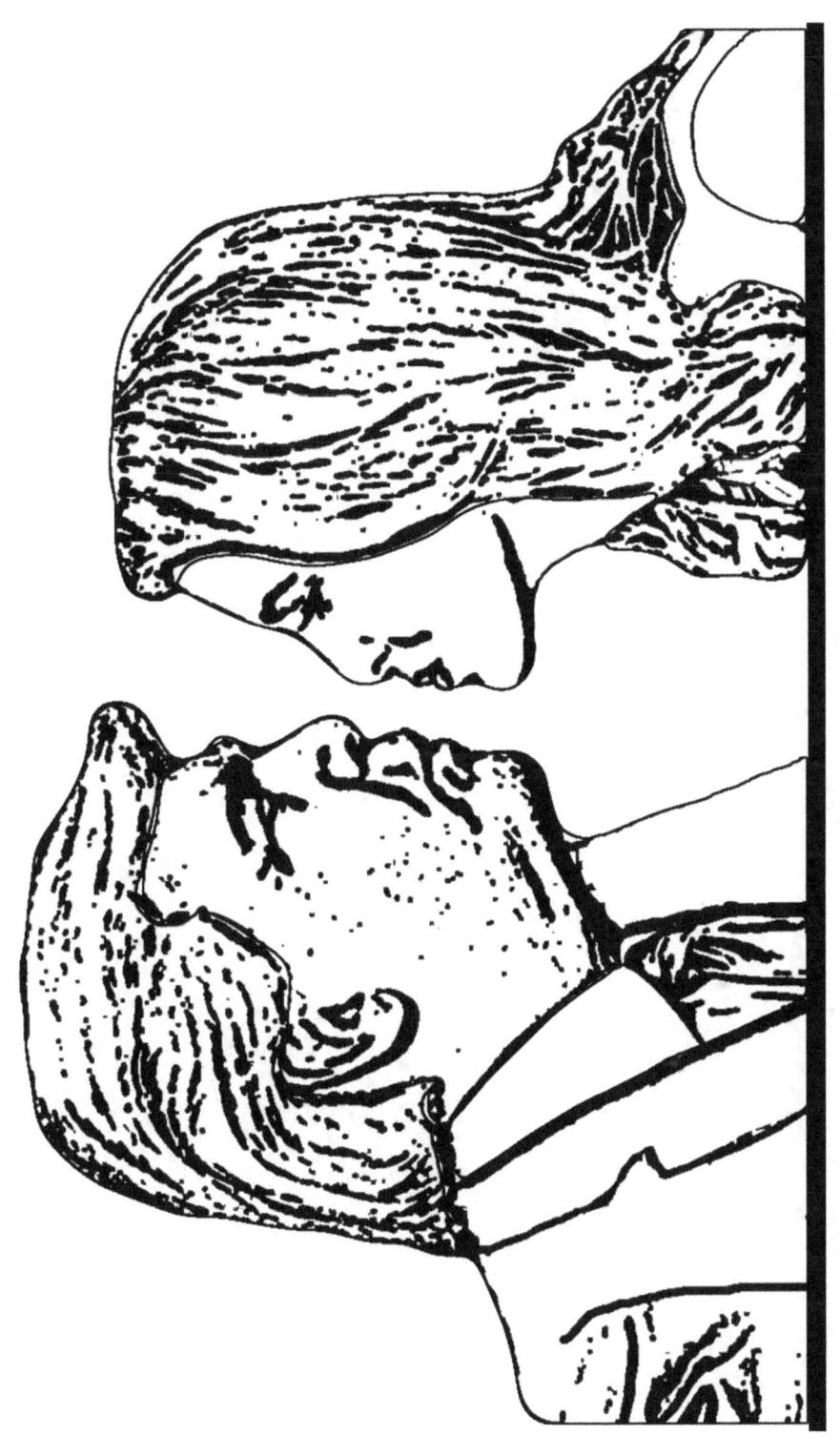

"I'VE SAID IF IVANKA WASN'T MY DAUGHTER PERHAPS I'D BE DATING HER"

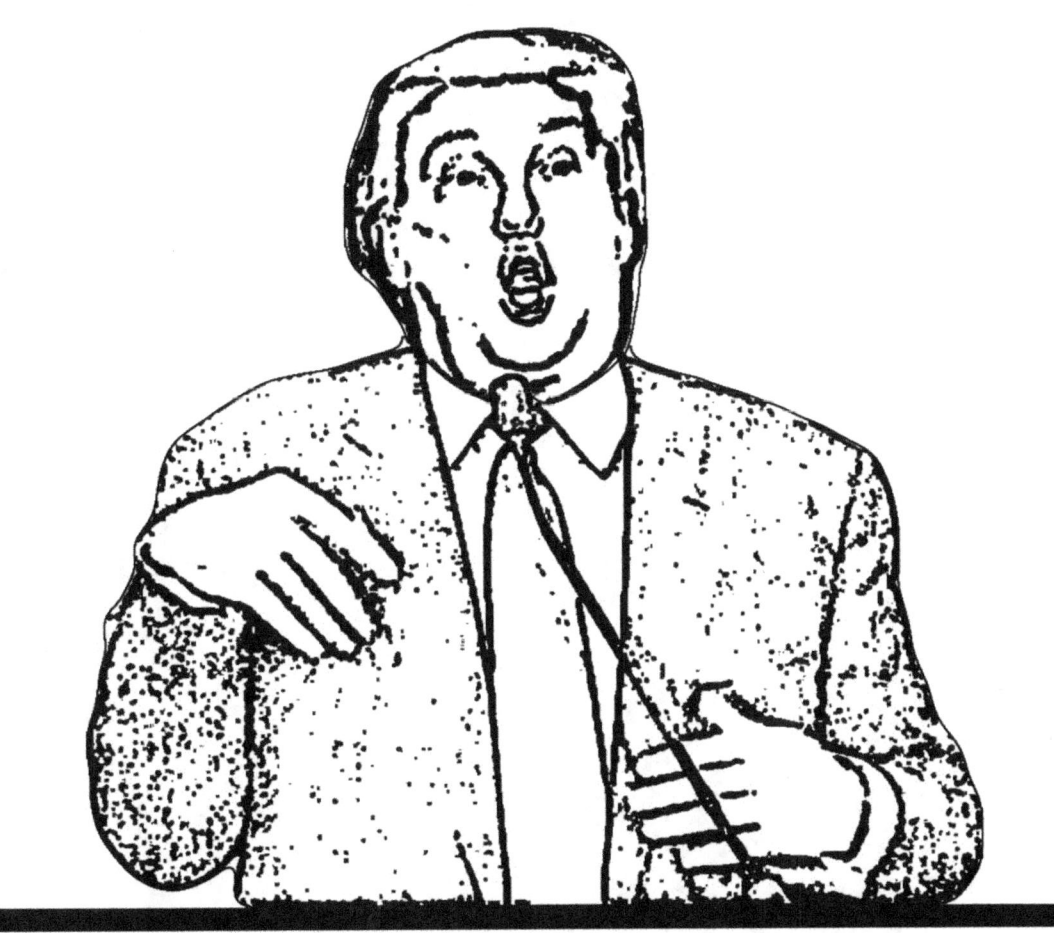

"My IQ is one of the highest —
and you all know it!
Please don't feel so stupid or
insecure; it's not your fault."

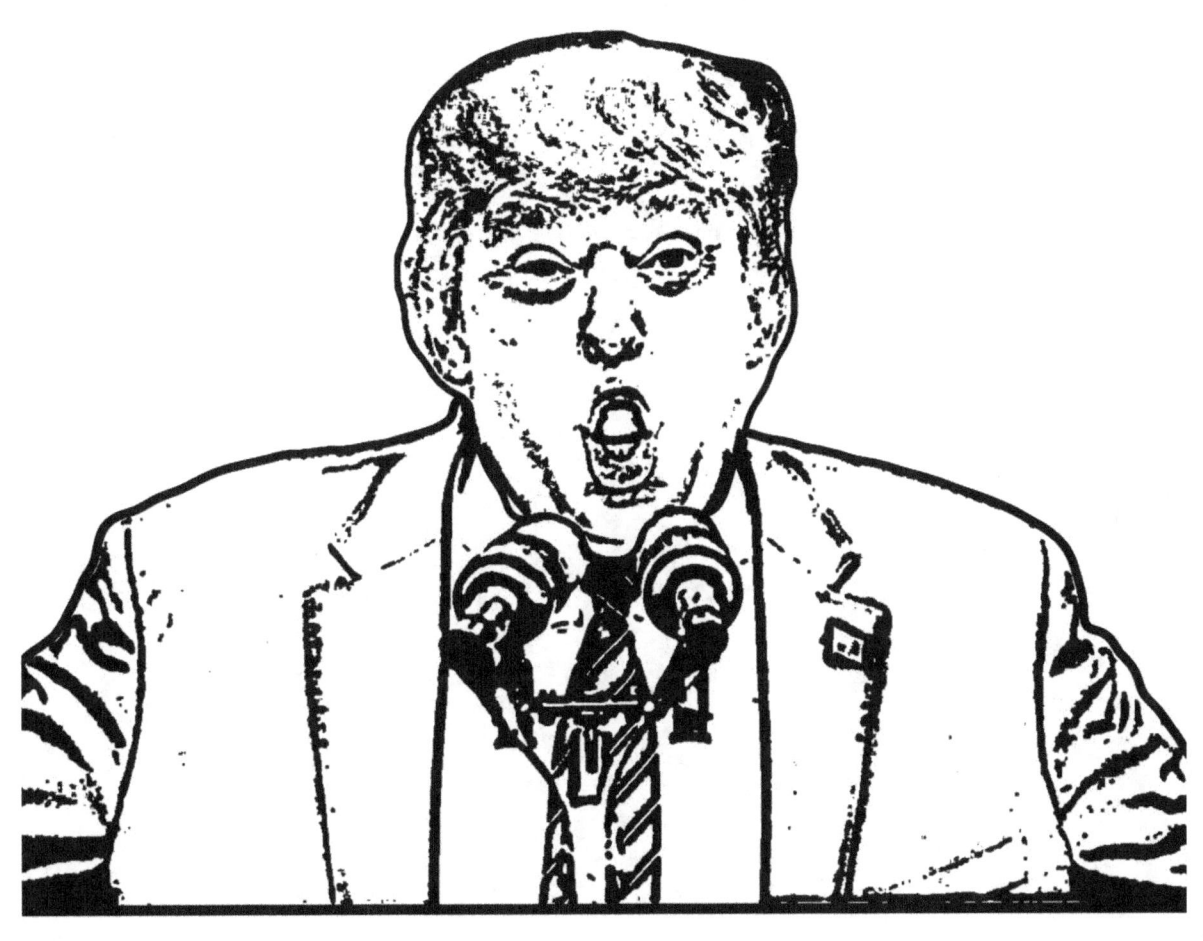

"IT'S FREEZING AND SNOWING
IN NEW YORK – WE NEED
GLOBAL WARMING!"

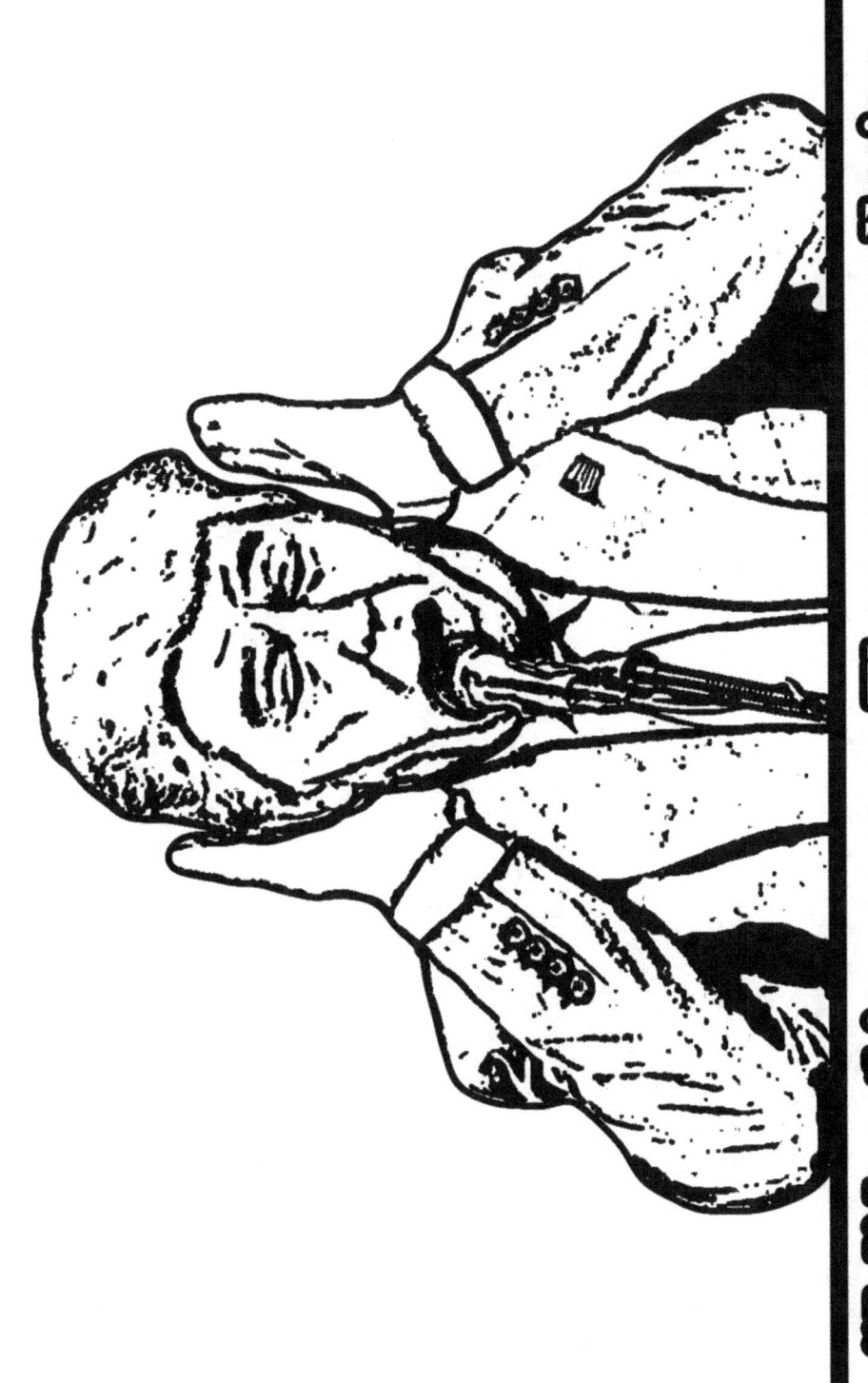

"I did nothing wrong. There was no collusion. There was no obstruction."

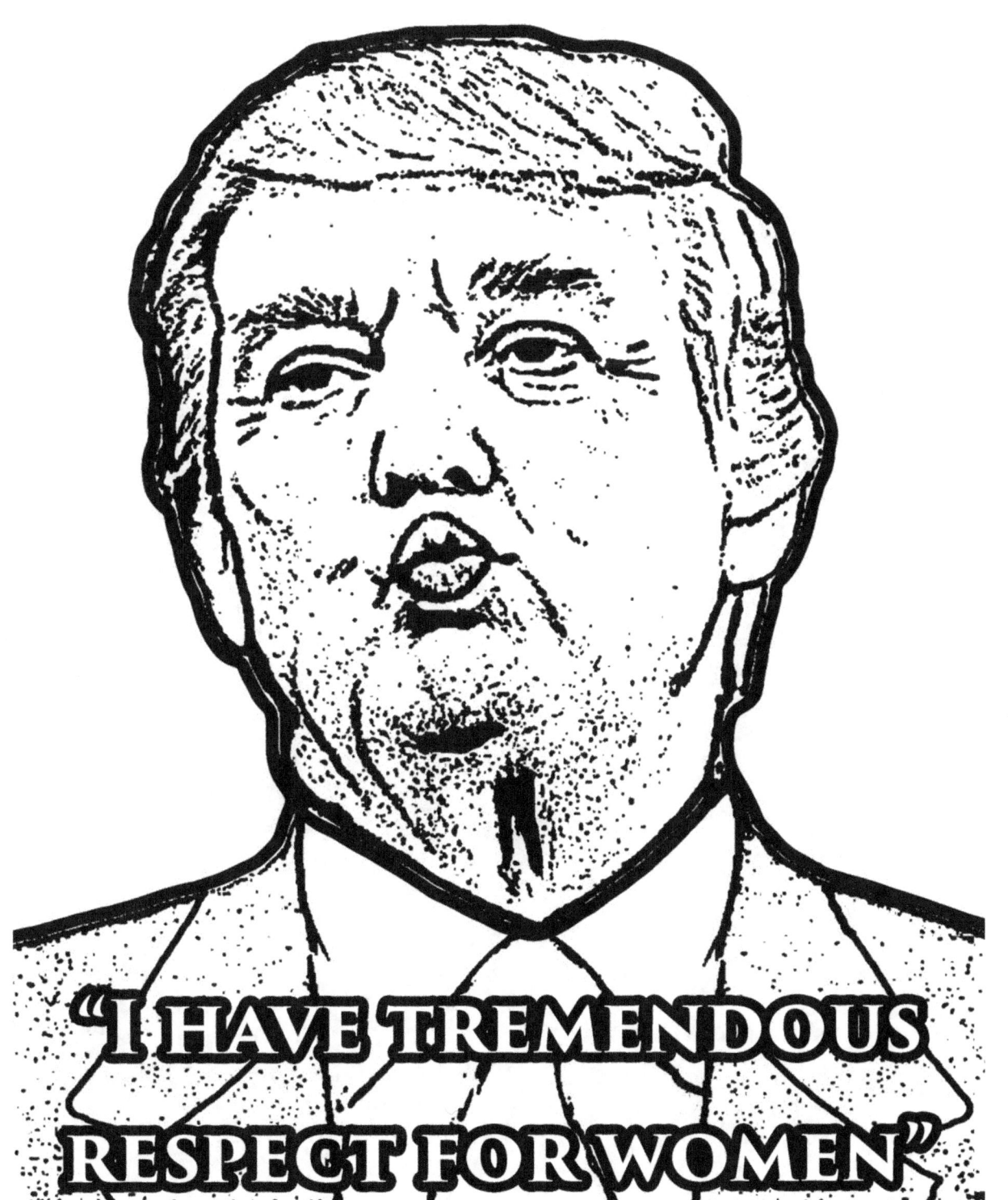

Days until > 50 %
disapproval:

President	Days
Reagan	727
Bush Sr.	1336
Clinton	573
Bush Jr.	1205
Obama	936
Trump	8

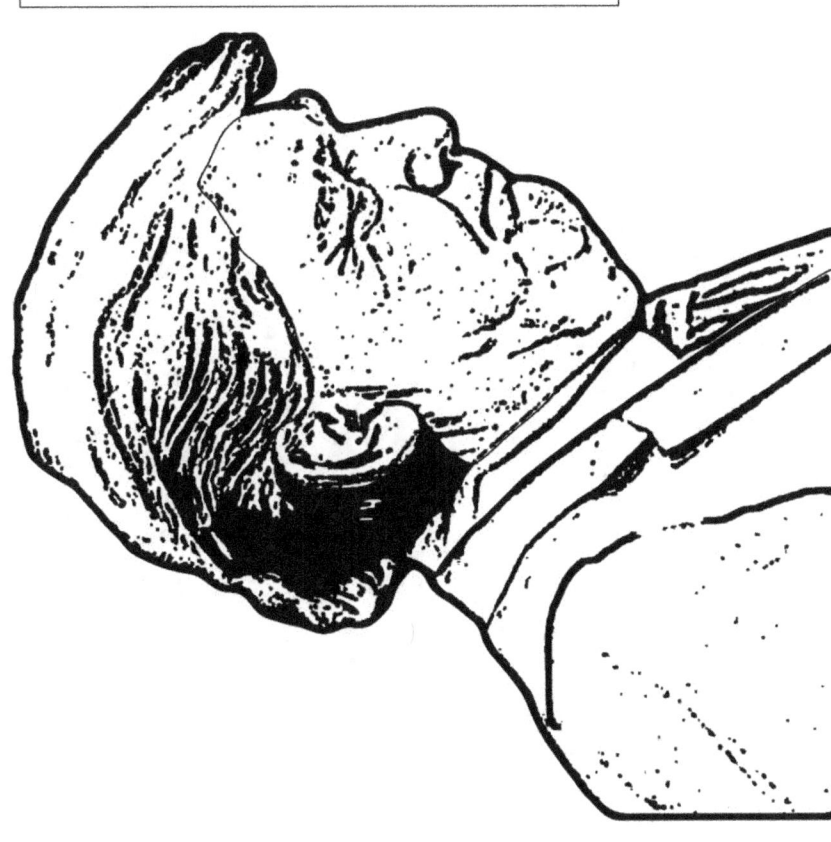

"We're going to win so much, you're going to be so sick and tired of winning" - Donald J. Trump

"Wouldn't you love to see one of these NFL owners, when somebody disrespects our flag, to say, 'Get that son of a bitch off the field right now. Out! He's fired. He's fired!'"

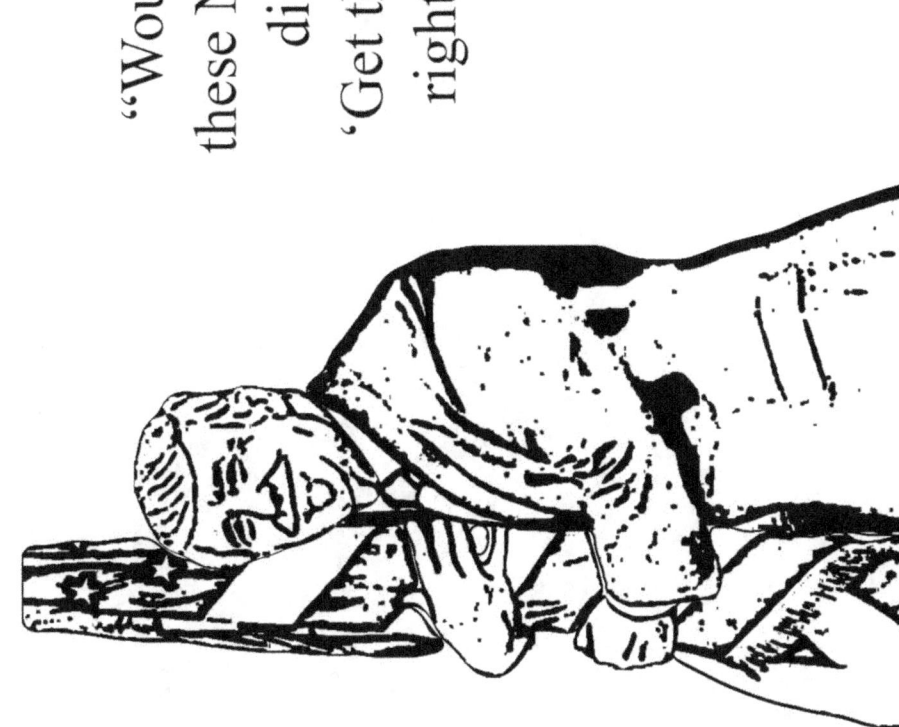

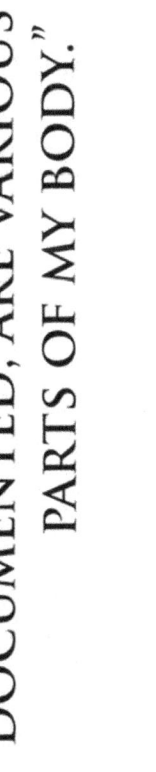

"MY FINGERS ARE LONG AND BEAUTIFUL, AS, IT HAS BEEN WELL DOCUMENTED, ARE VARIOUS OTHER PARTS OF MY BODY."

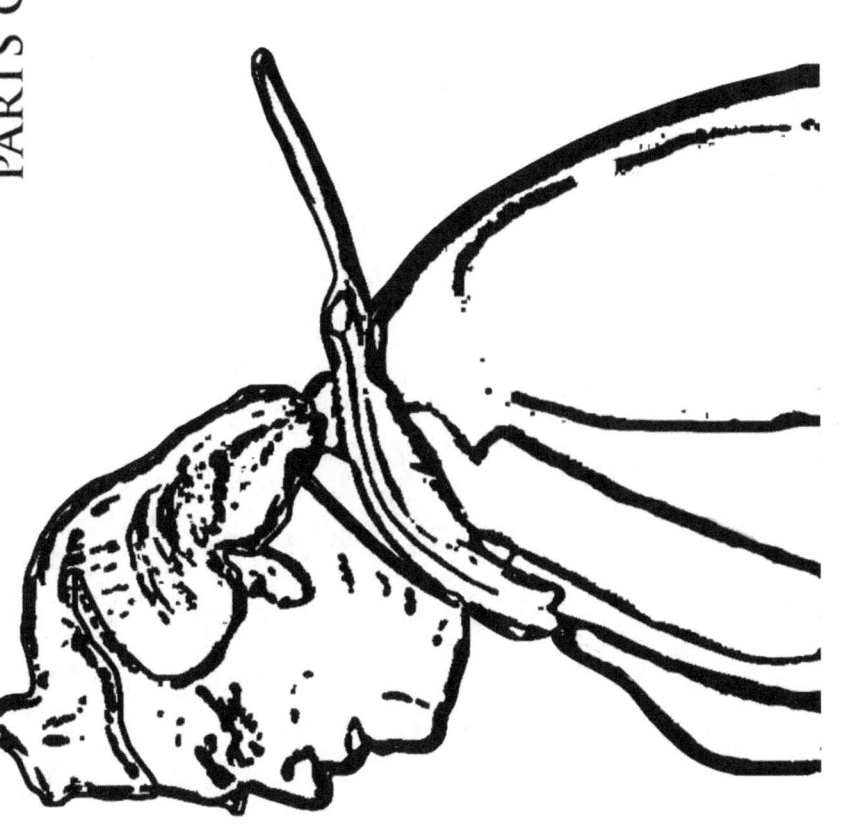

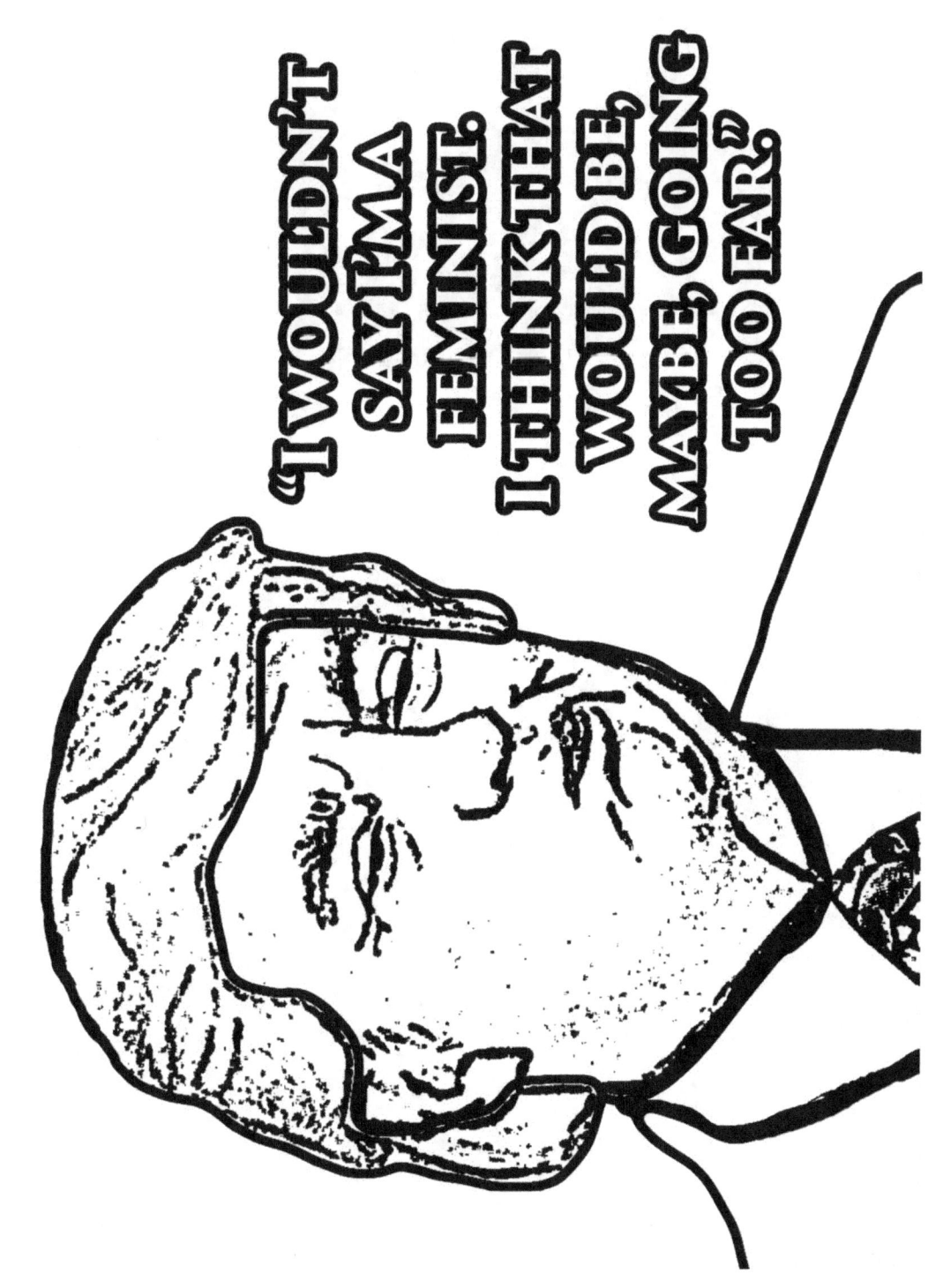

"I WOULDN'T SAY I'M A FEMINIST. I THINK THAT WOULD BE, MAYBE, GOING TOO FAR."

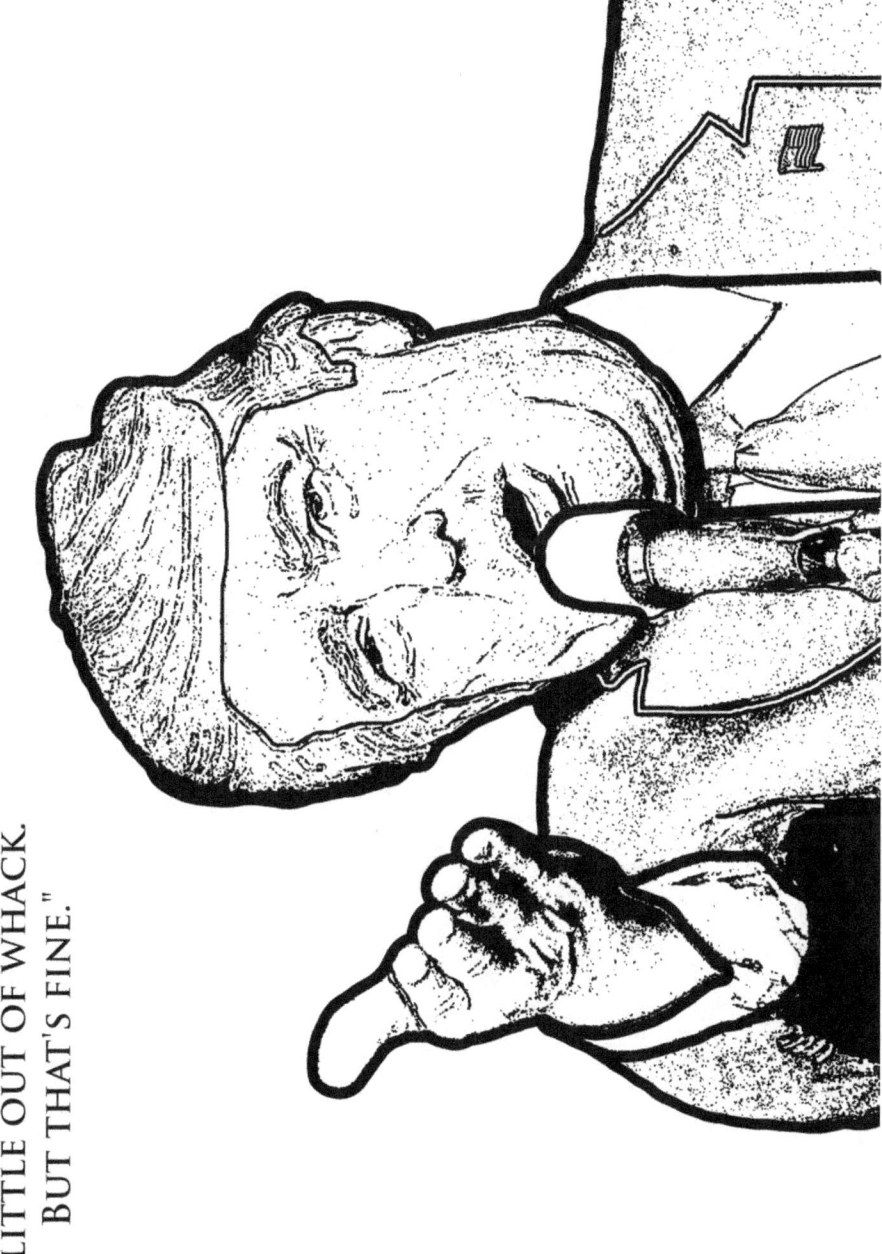

In reference to Hurricane Maria's devastation...
"I HATE TO TELL YOU, PUERTO RICO,
BUT YOU THREW OUR BUDGET
A LITTLE OUT OF WHACK.
BUT THAT'S FINE."

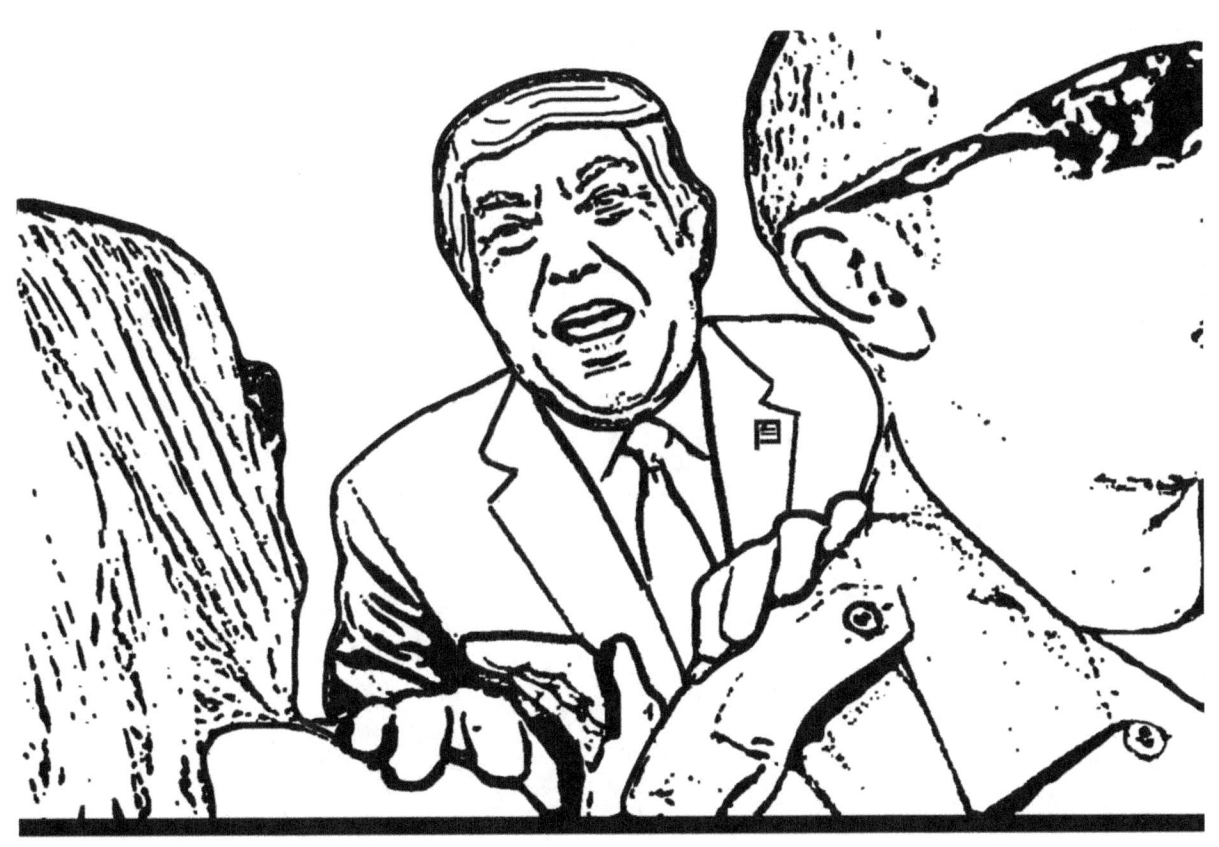

"You know, I'm automatically
attracted to beautiful - I just start kissing them.
It's like a magnet. Just kiss.
I don't even wait.
And when you're a star, they let you do it.
You can do anything...
Grab them by the pussy.
You can do anything."

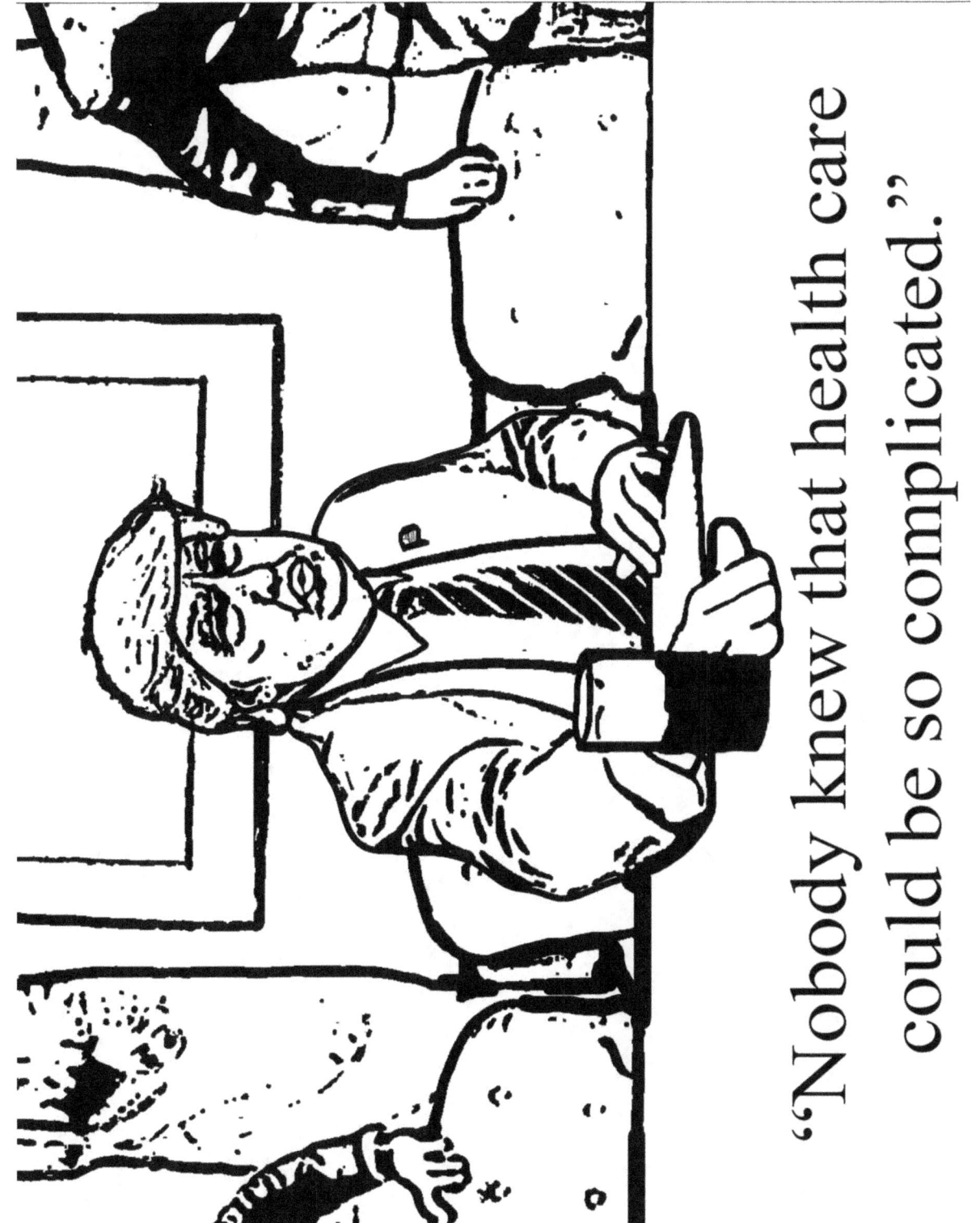

"Nobody knew that health care could be so complicated."

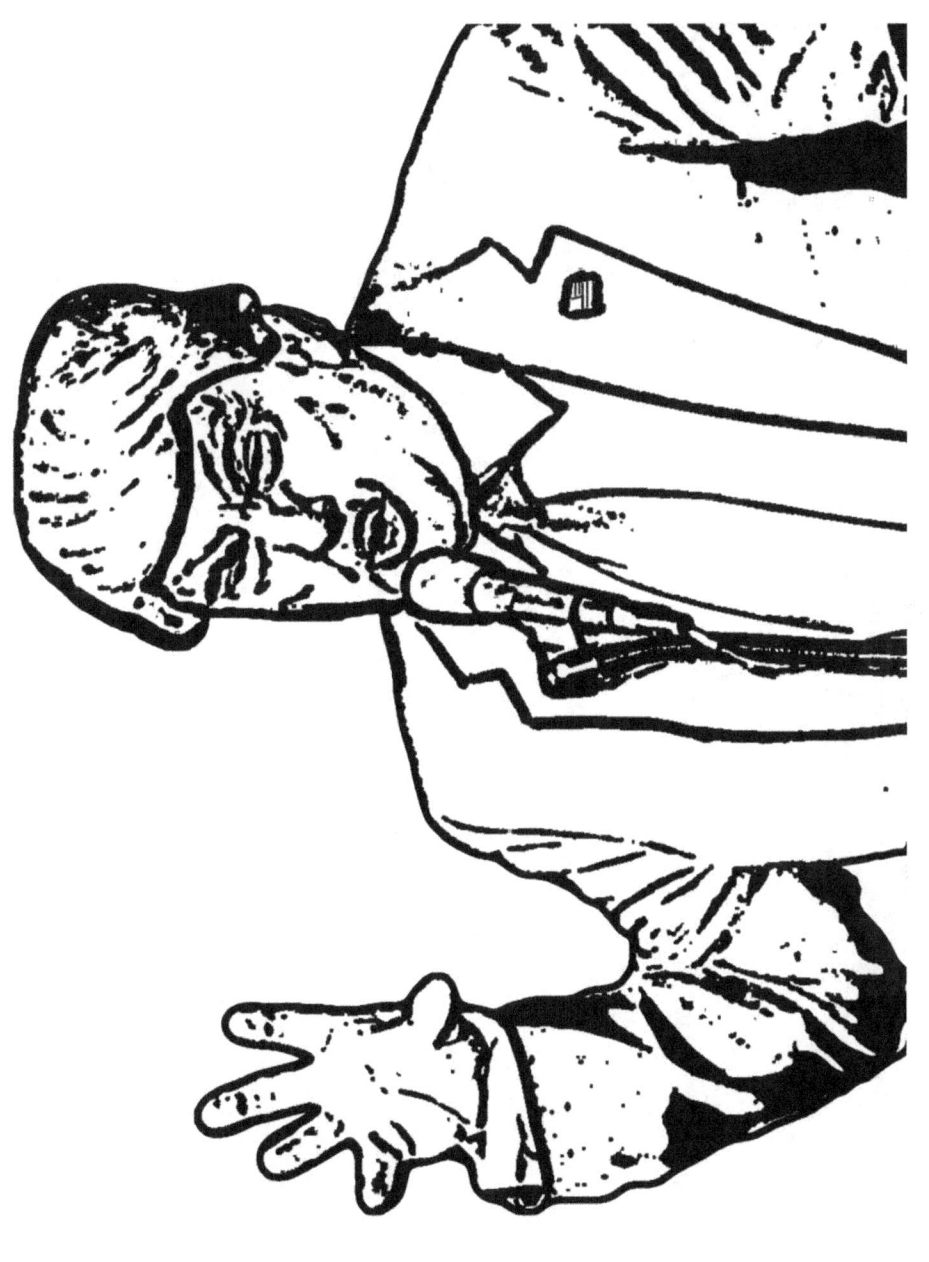

"I WAS DOWN THERE, AND I WATCHED OUR POLICE AND OUR FIREMEN, DOWN ON 7-ELEVEN, DOWN AT THE WORLD TRADE CENTER, RIGHT AFTER IT CAME DOWN"

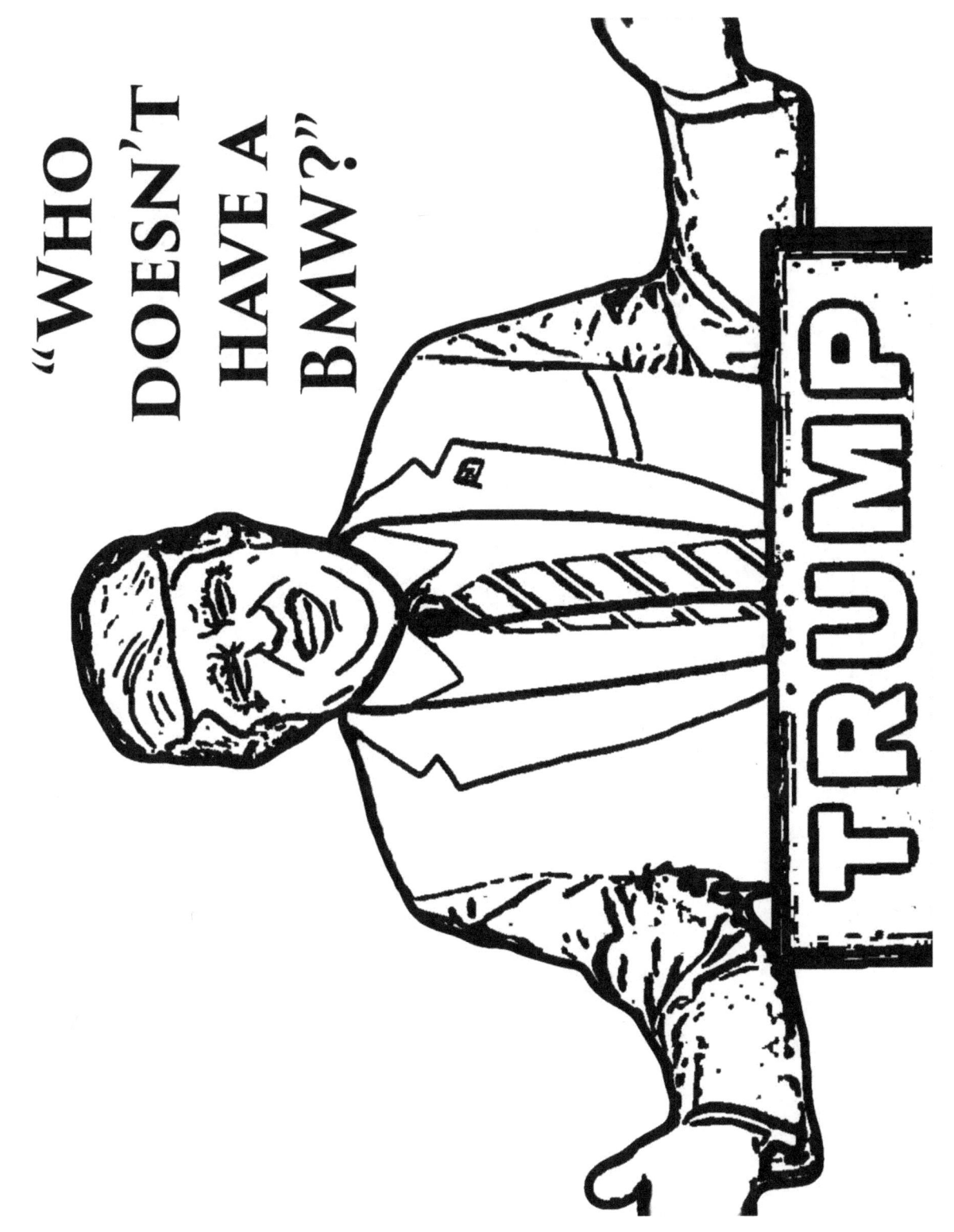

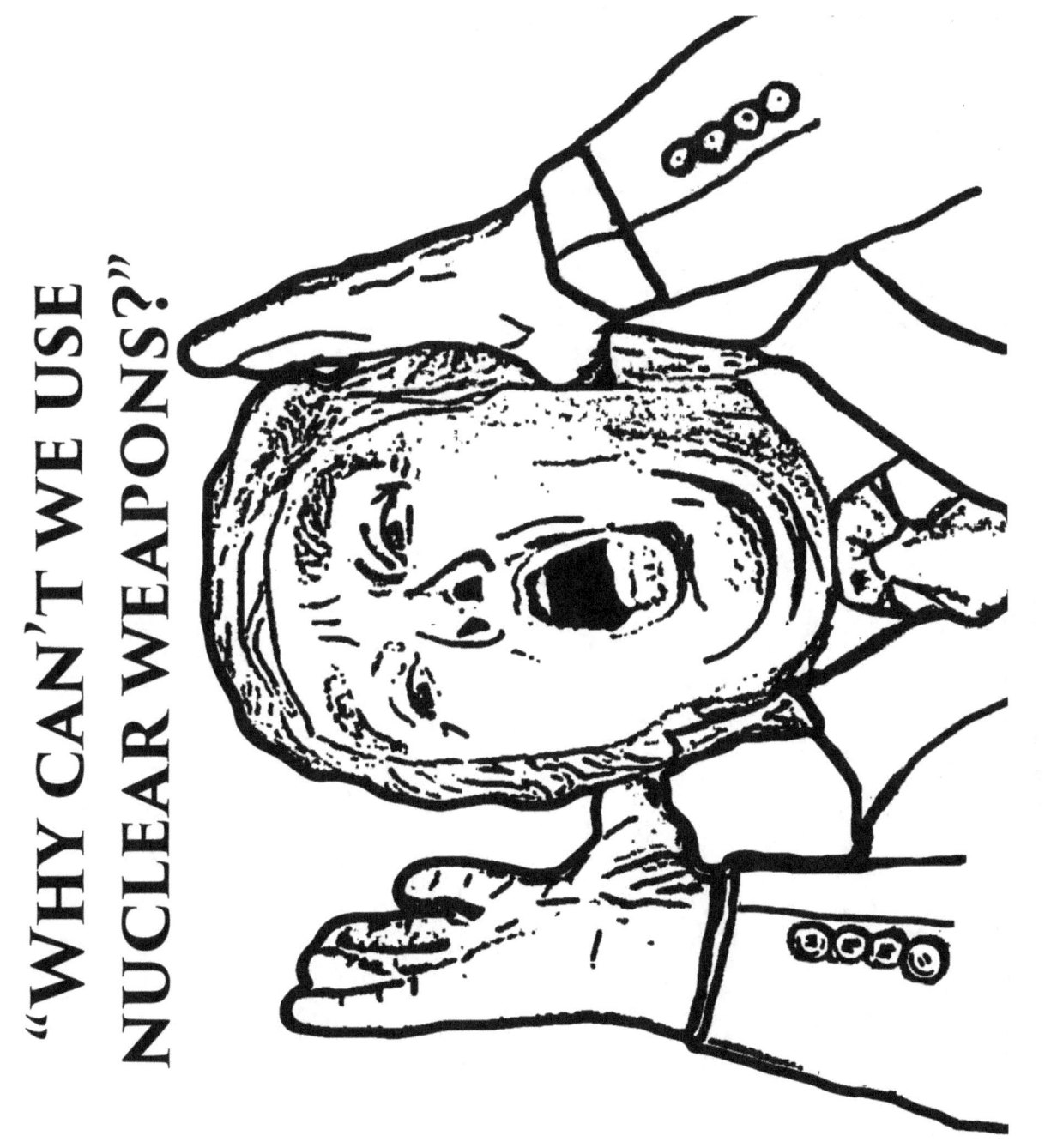

"WHY CAN'T WE USE NUCLEAR WEAPONS?"

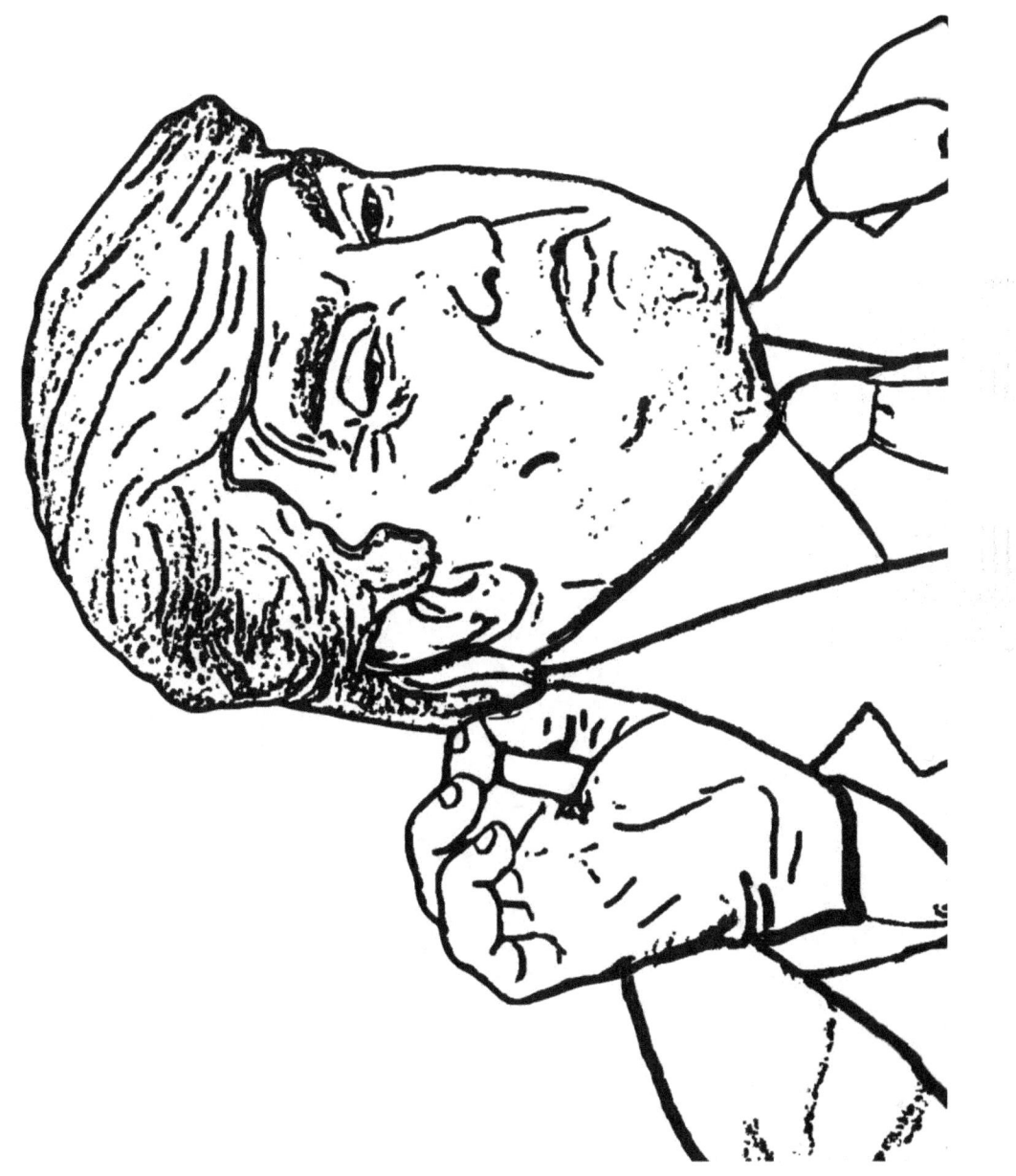

"I THINK I AM ACTUALLY HUMBLE. I THINK I'M MUCH MORE HUMBLE THAN YOU WOULD UNDERSTAND."

"Actually, throughout my life, my two greatest assets have been mental stability and being, like, really smart"

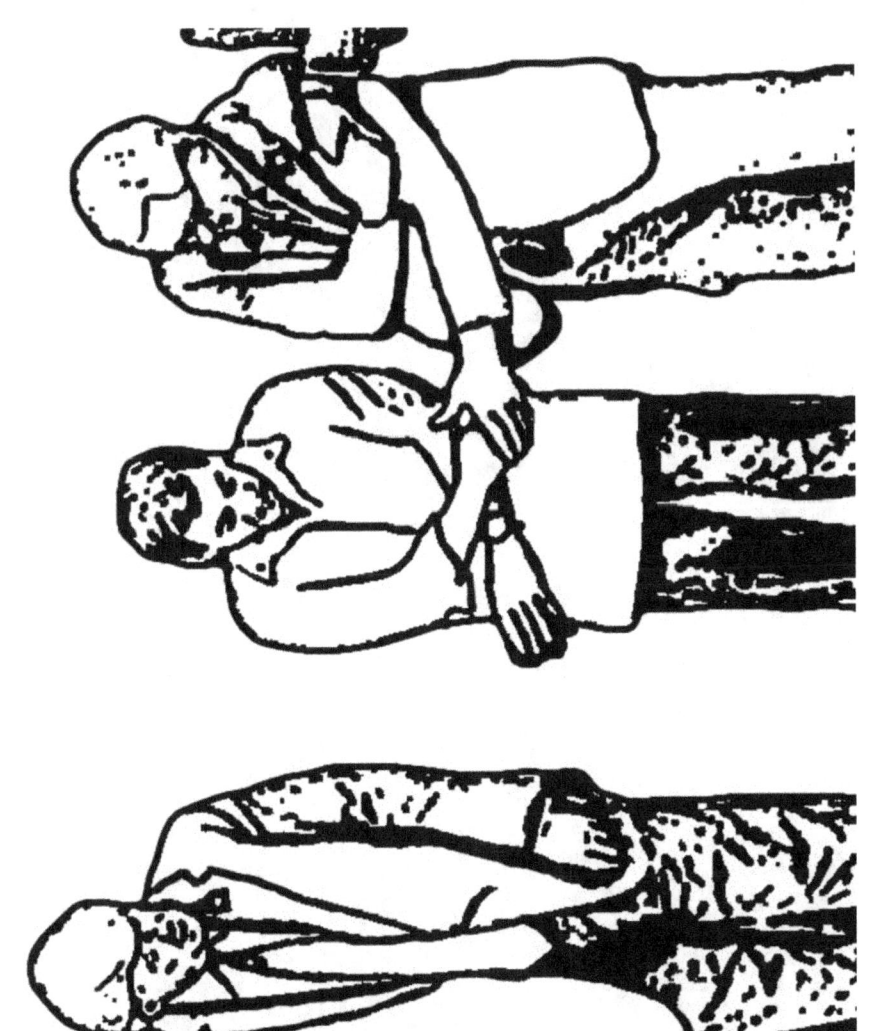
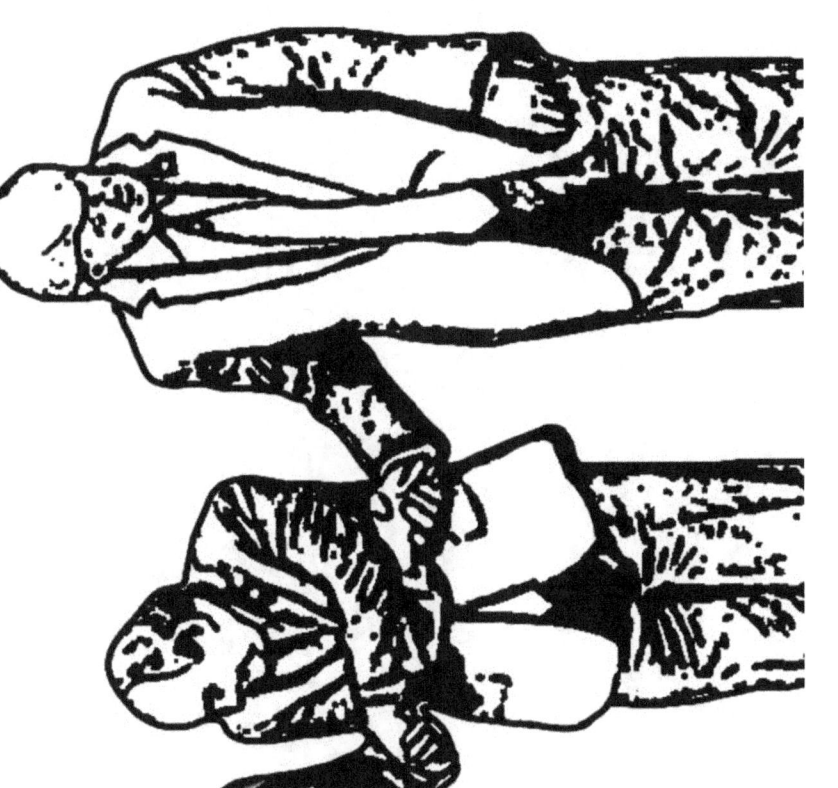

"Steve Bannon has nothing to do with me or my Presidency, okay, I'm not even sure who he is."

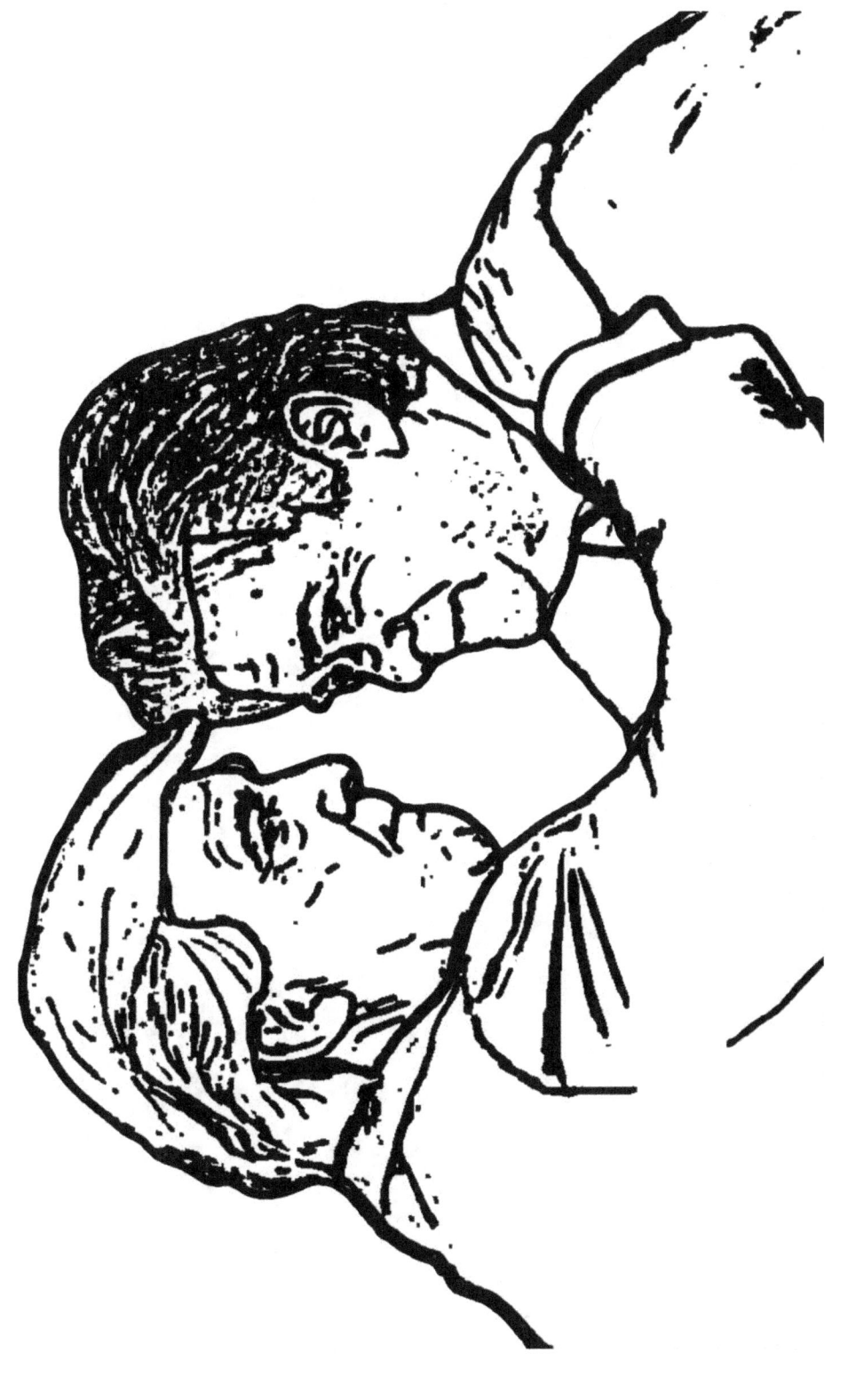

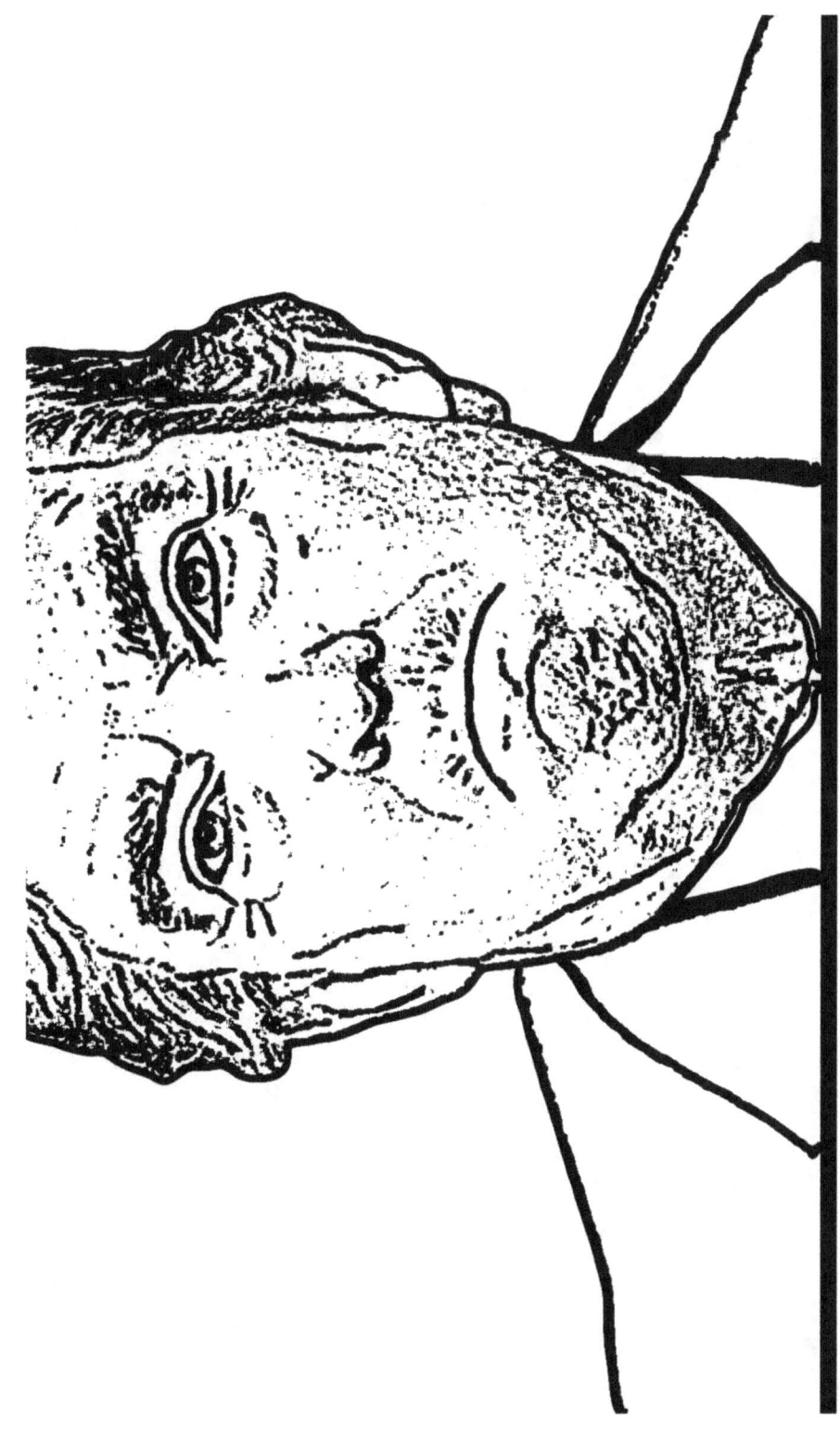

"ROBERT PATTINSON SHOULD NOT TAKE BACK KRISTEN STEWART. SHE CHEATED ON HIM LIKE A DOG & WILL DO IT AGAIN – JUST WATCH. HE CAN DO MUCH BETTER!"

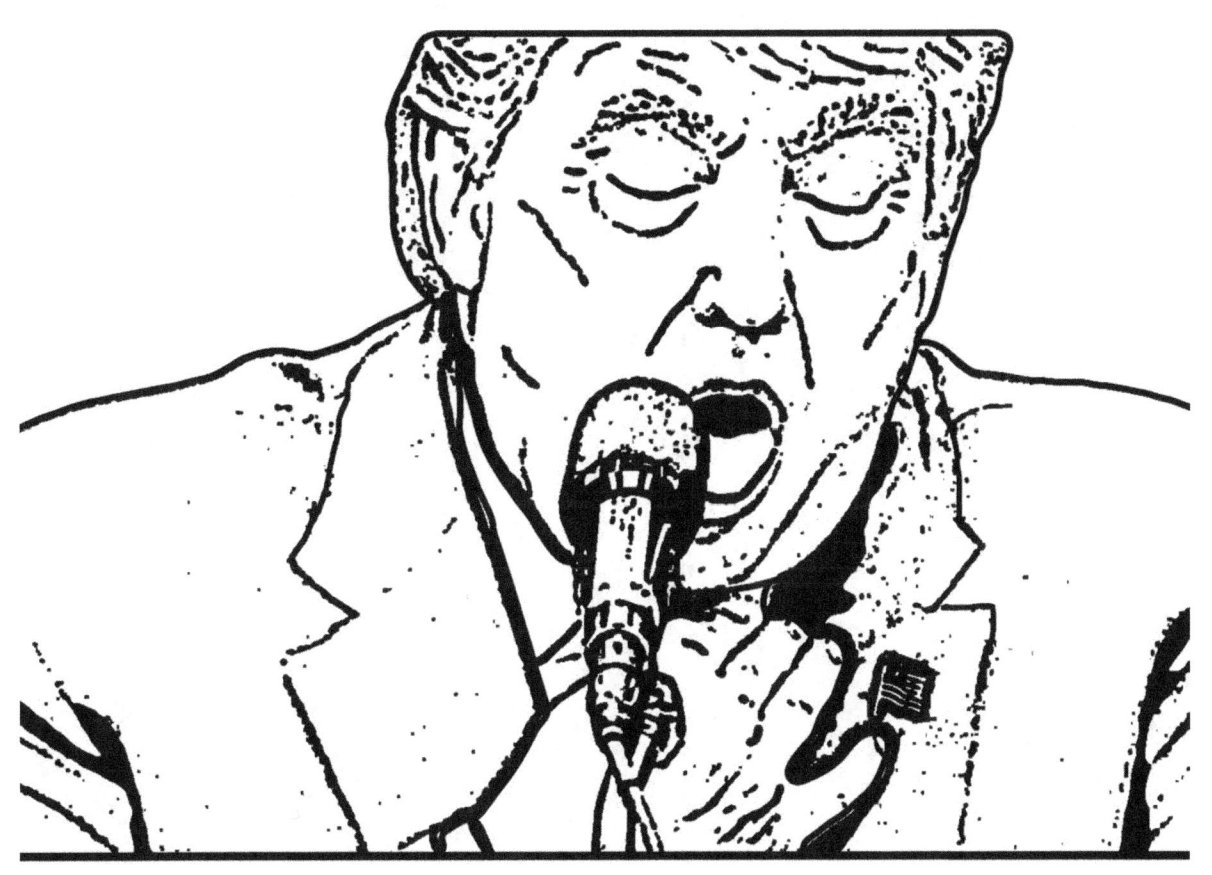

"I consider my health, stamina and strength one of my greatest assets. The world has watched me for many years and can so testify - great genes!"

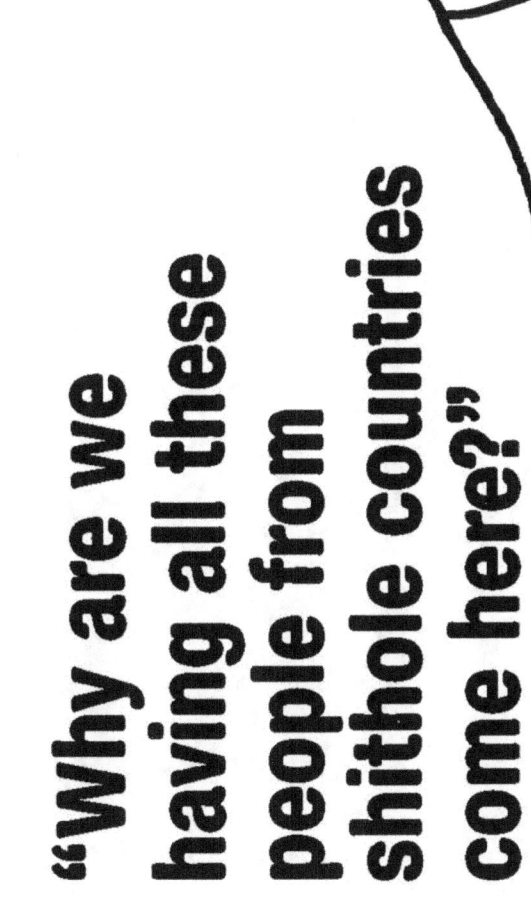

"Why are we having all these people from shithole countries come here?"

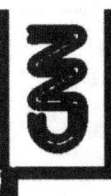

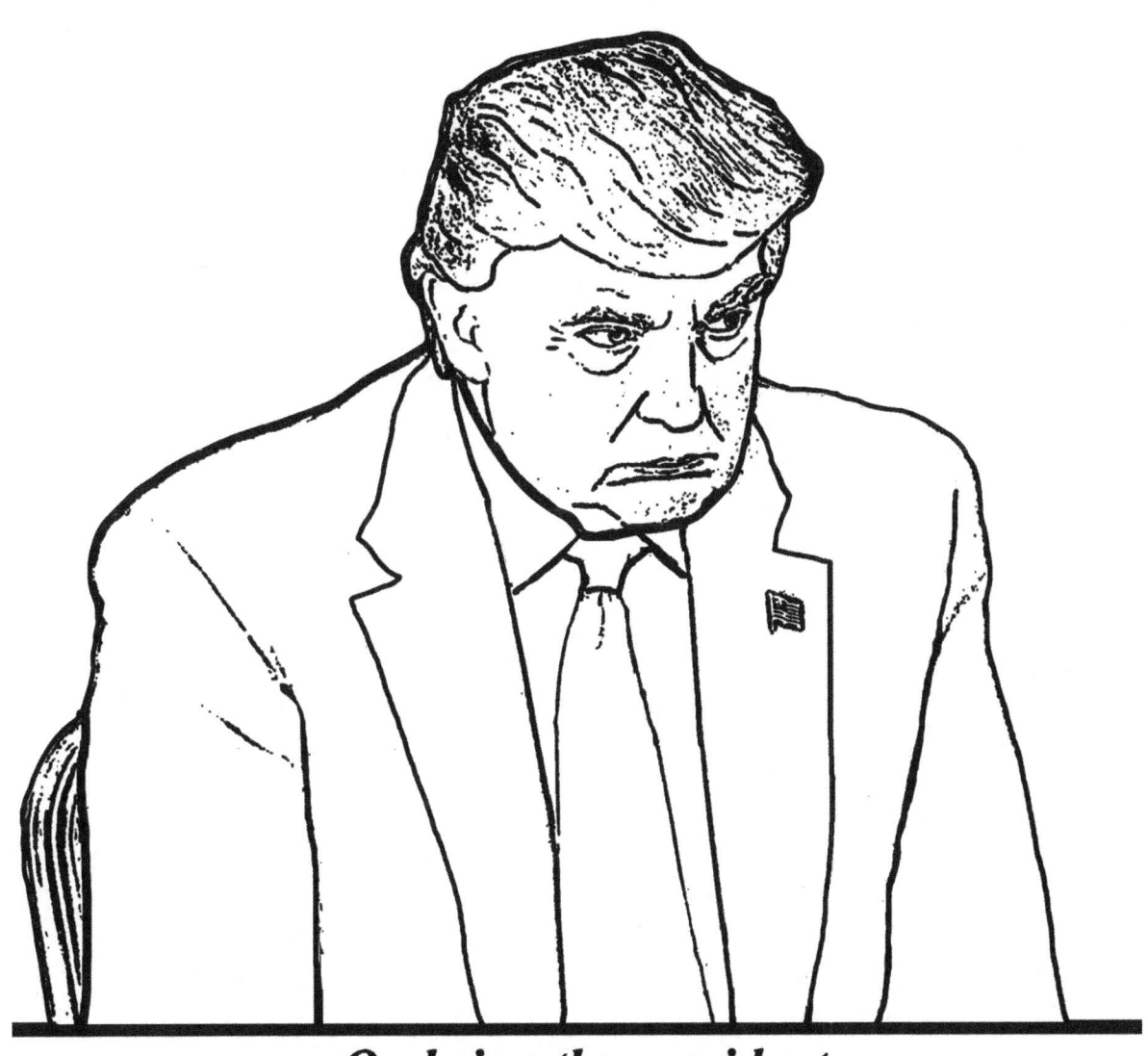

On being the president:
"THIS IS MORE WORK THAN IN MY
PREVIOUS LIFE.
I THOUGHT IT WOULD BE EASIER."

In reference to G7 and the annexation of Crimea...

**"Some people like the idea of bringing Russia back in...
And something happened a while ago, where Russia is no
longer in."**

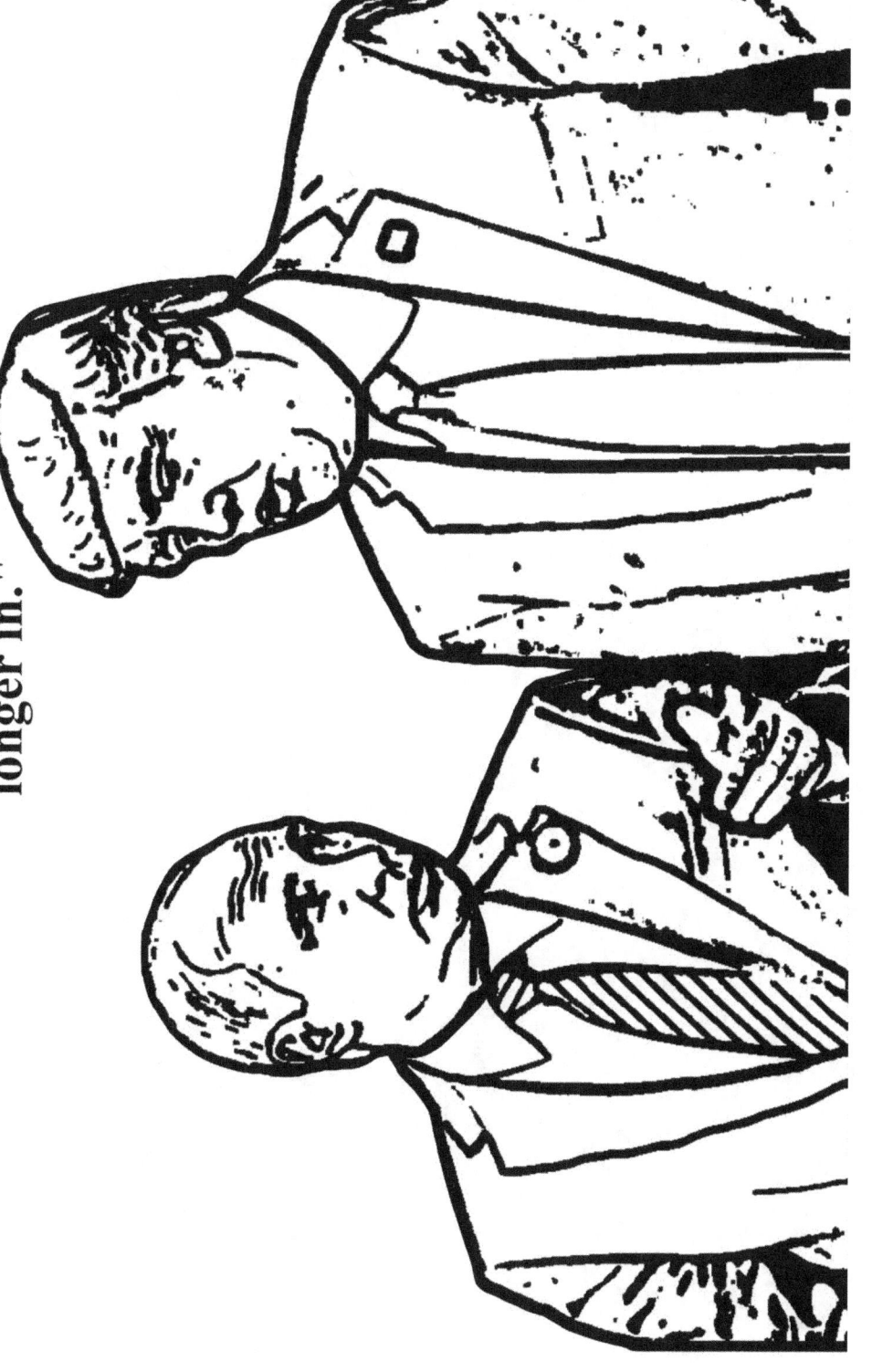

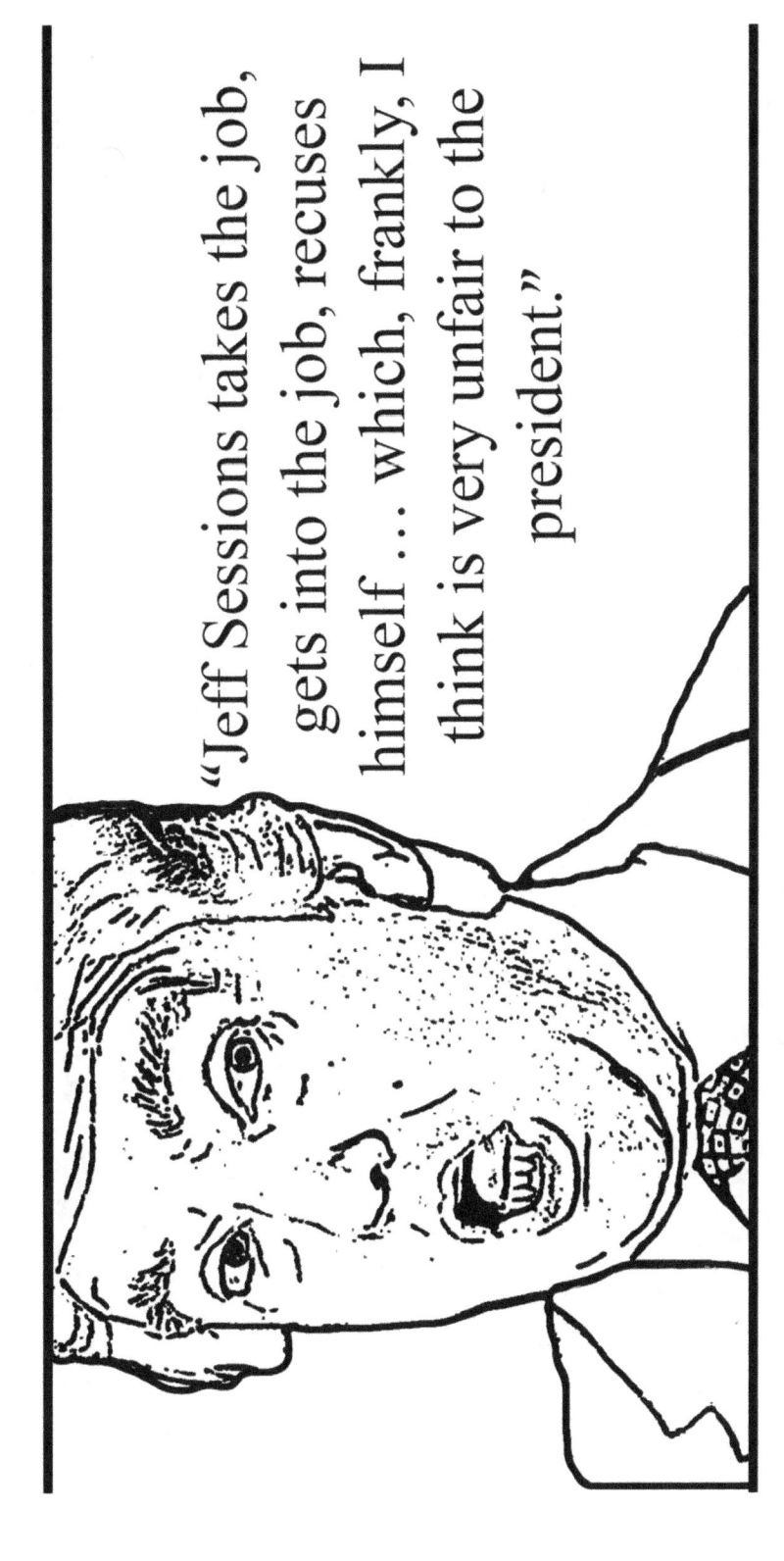

"Jeff Sessions takes the job, gets into the job, recuses himself ... which, frankly, I think is very unfair to the president."

"Look at those hands, are they small hands? And, [Marco Rubio] referred to my hands: 'If they're small, something else must be small.' I guarantee you there's no problem. I guarantee."

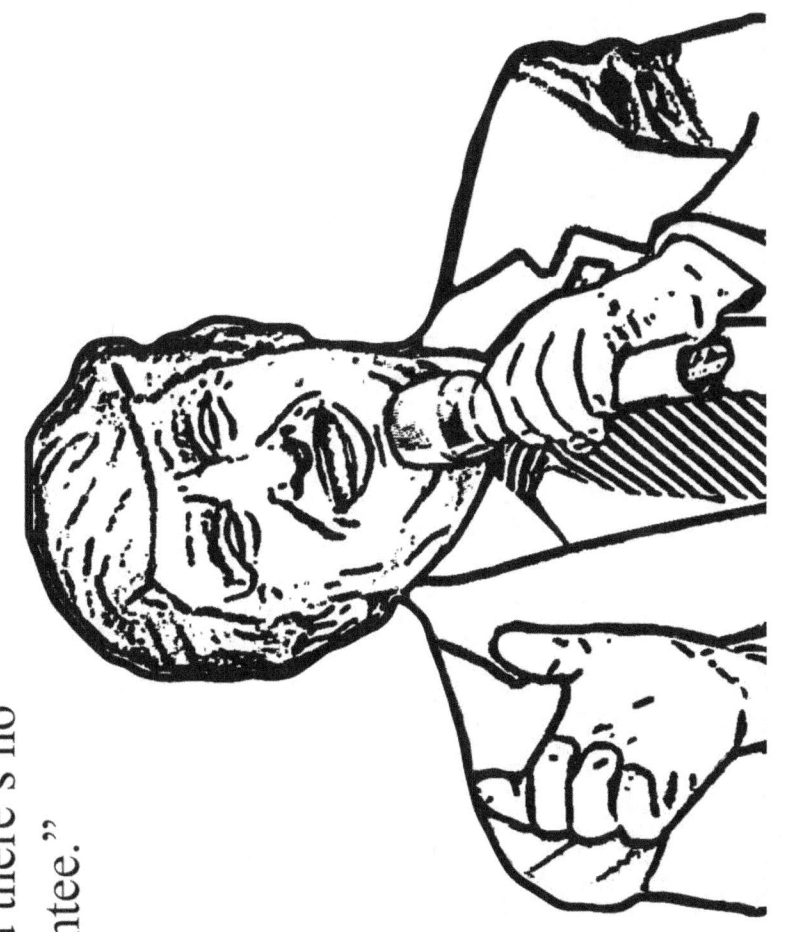

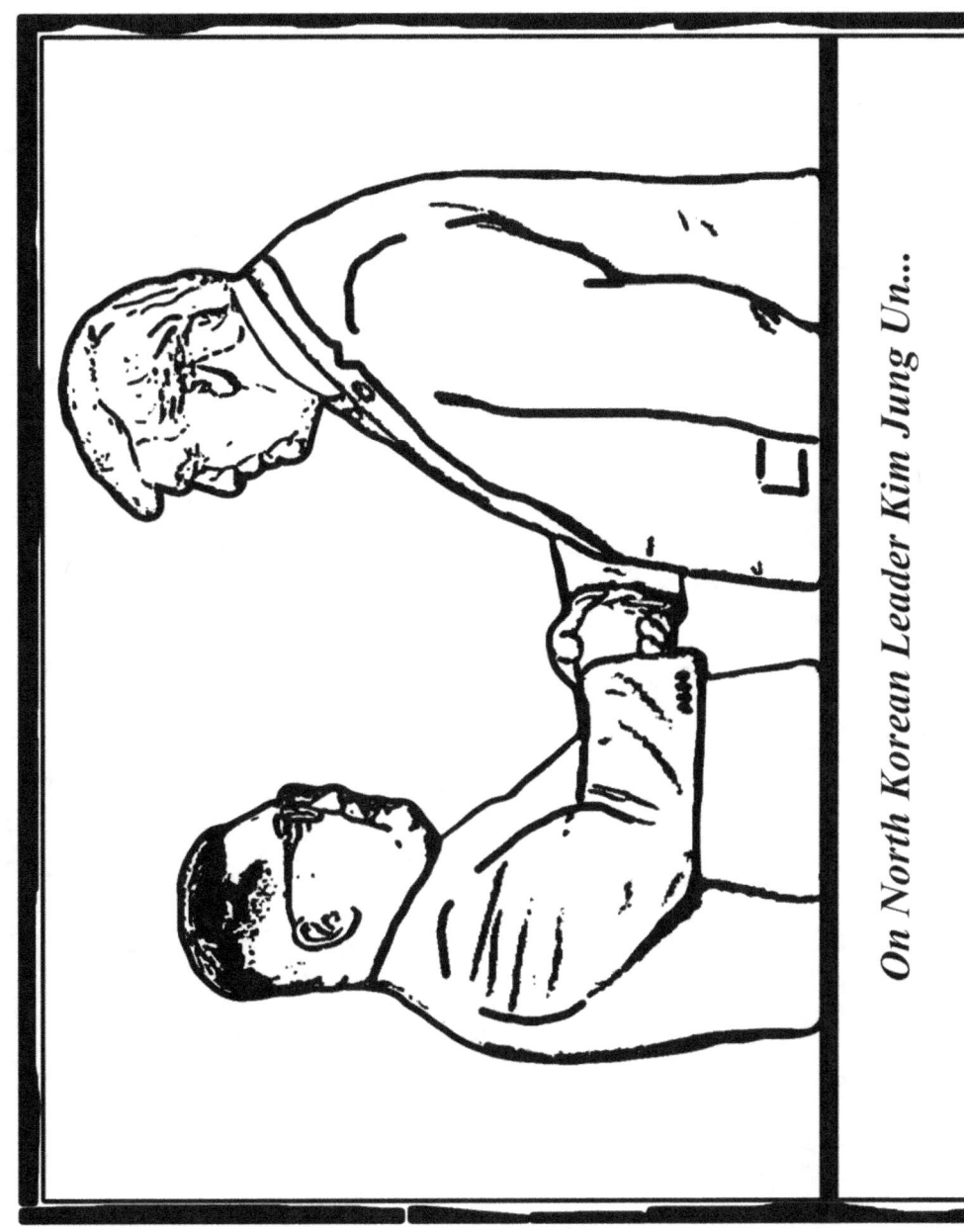

On North Korean Leader Kim Jung Un...

"HE SPEAKS AND HIS PEOPLE SIT UP AT ATTENTION, I WANT MY PEOPLE TO DO THE SAME."

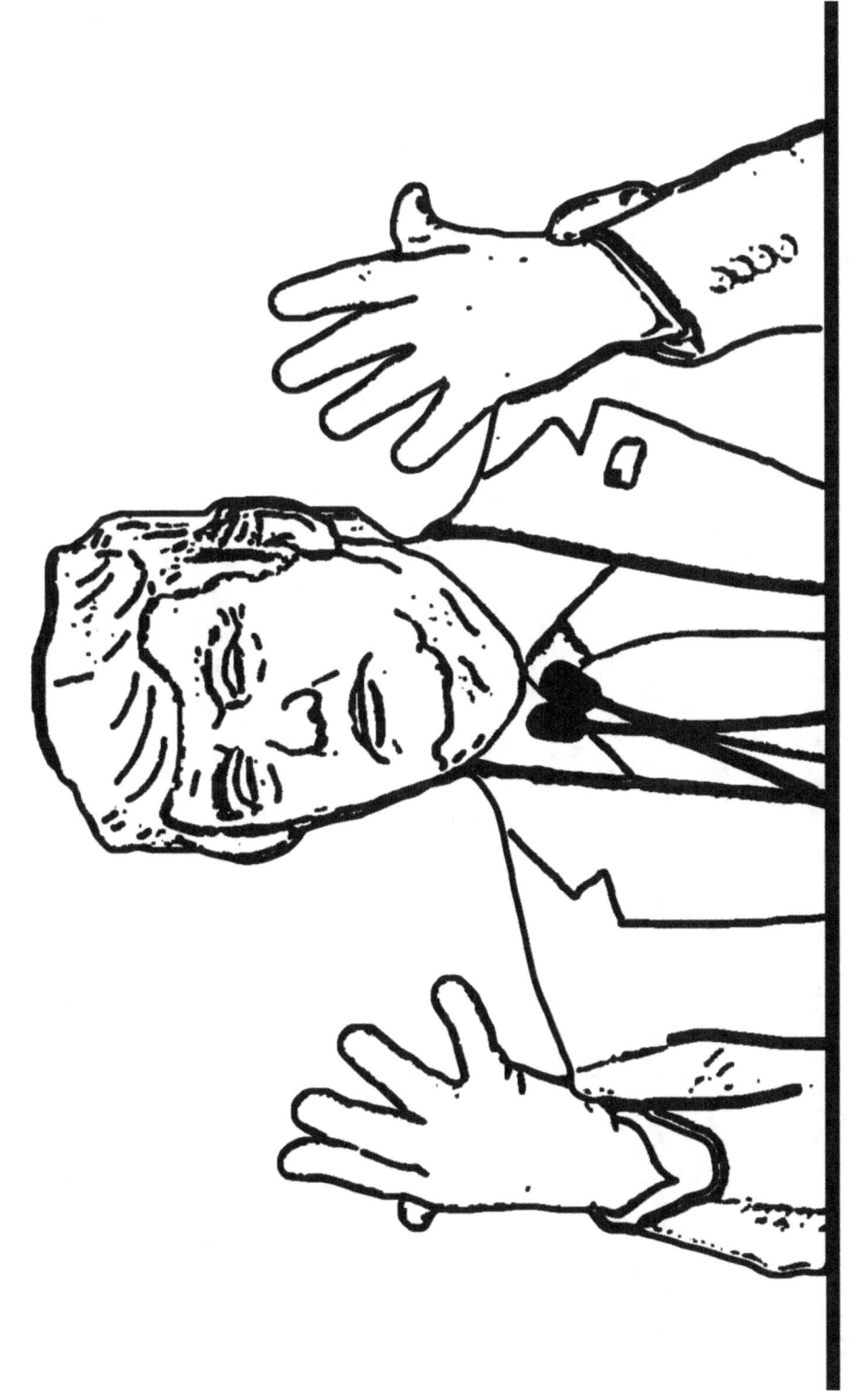

"Despite the constant negative press covfefe"

"I HAVE A VERY GOOD BRAIN AND I'VE SAID A LOT OF THINGS"

Photo from the August 21, 2017 solar eclipse

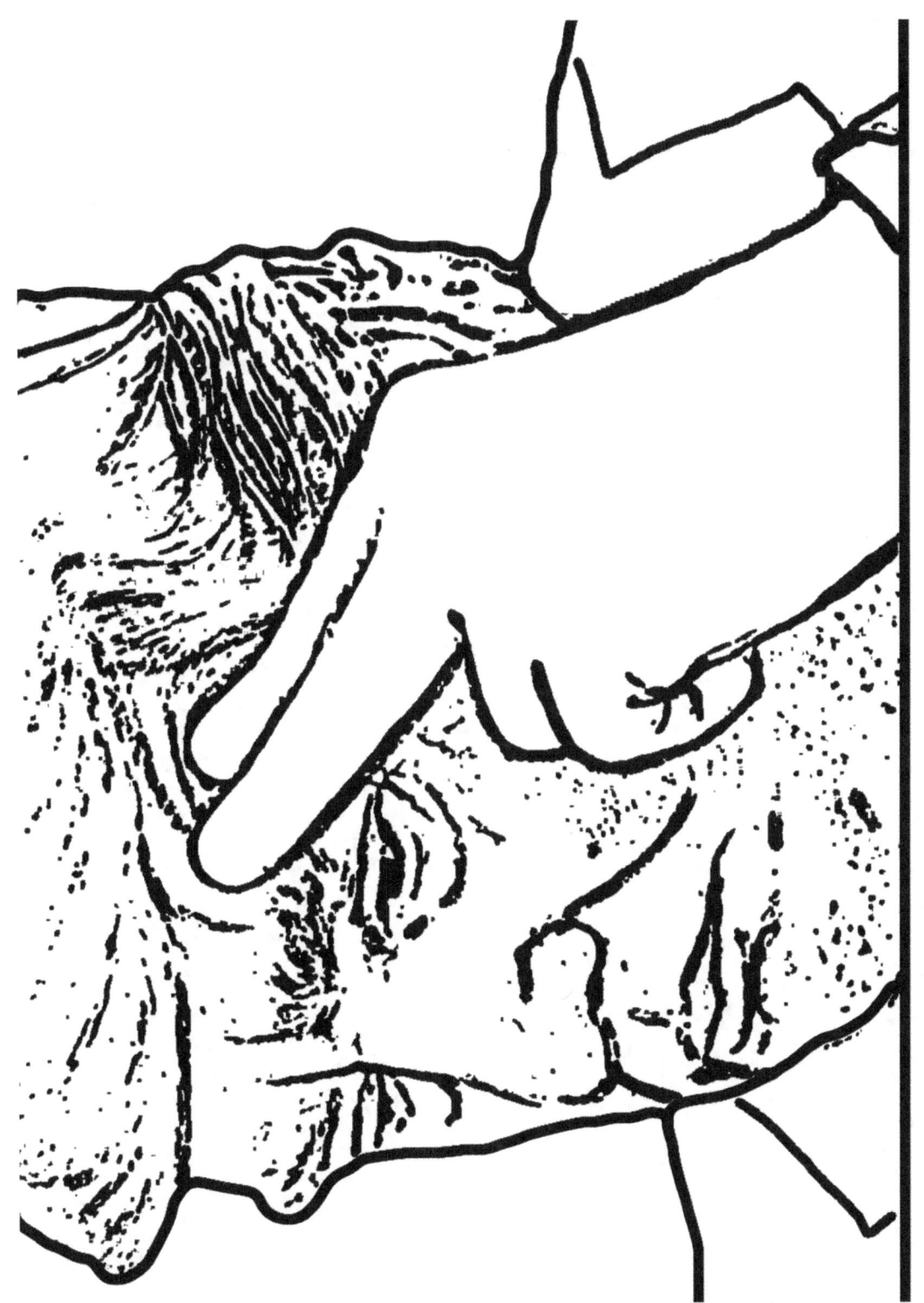

"I have one of the great memories of all time."

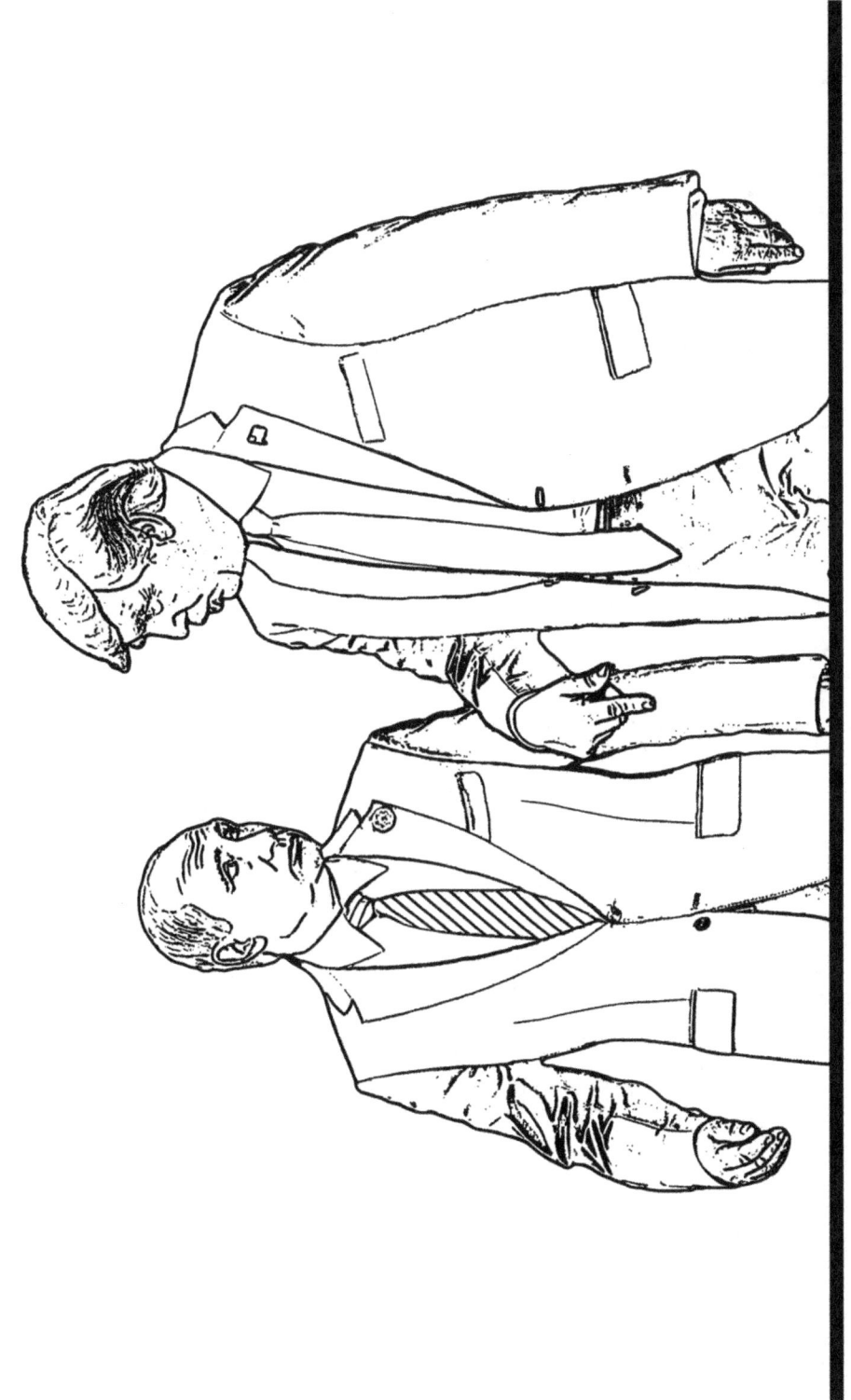

In response to Bill O'Reilly calling Putin 'a killer'...

"THERE ARE A LOT OF KILLERS, DO YOU THINK OUR COUNTRY IS SO INNOCENT?
DO YOU THINK OUR COUNTRY IS SO INNOCENT?"

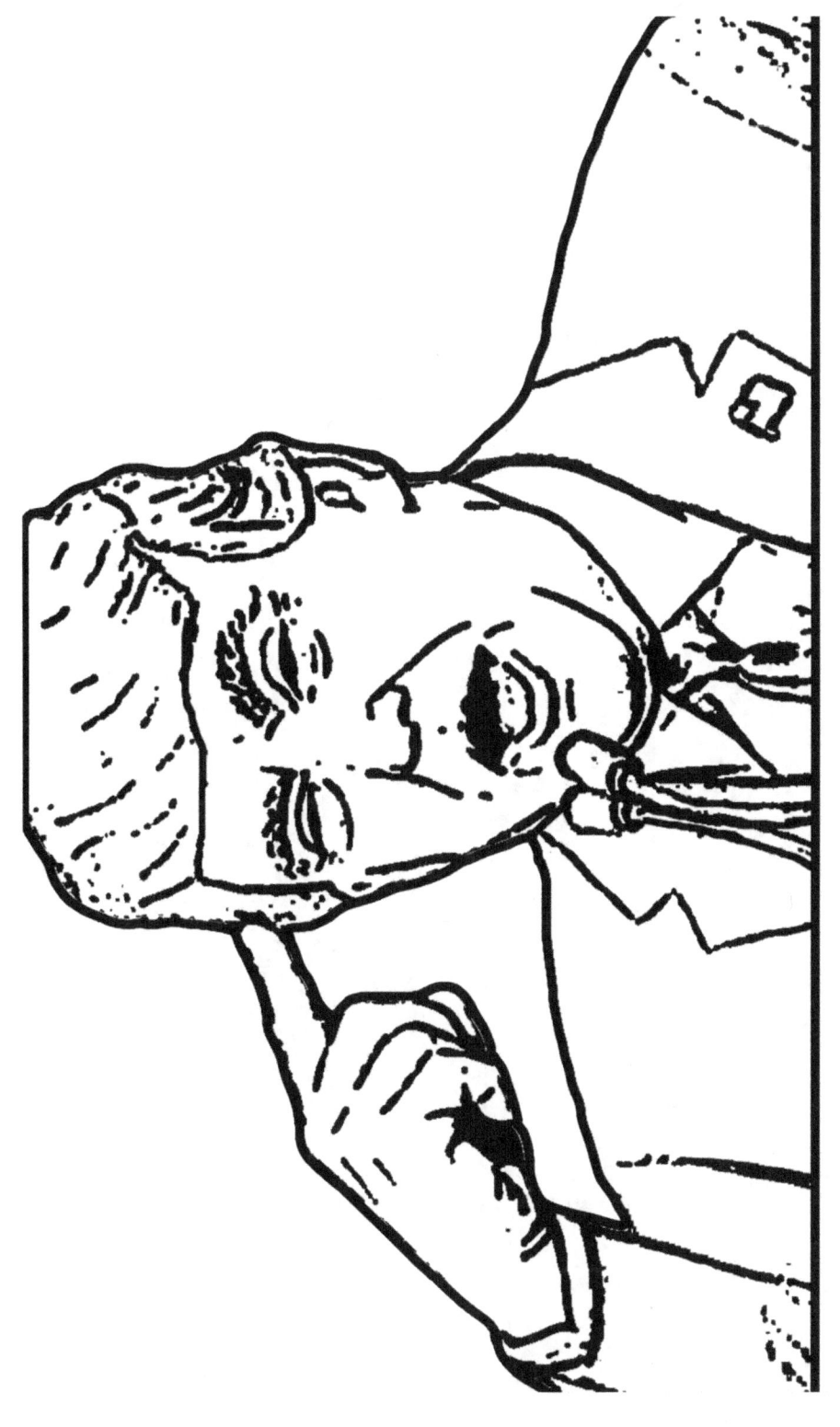

"Nobody has better respect for intelligence than Donald Trump."

Donald Trump.

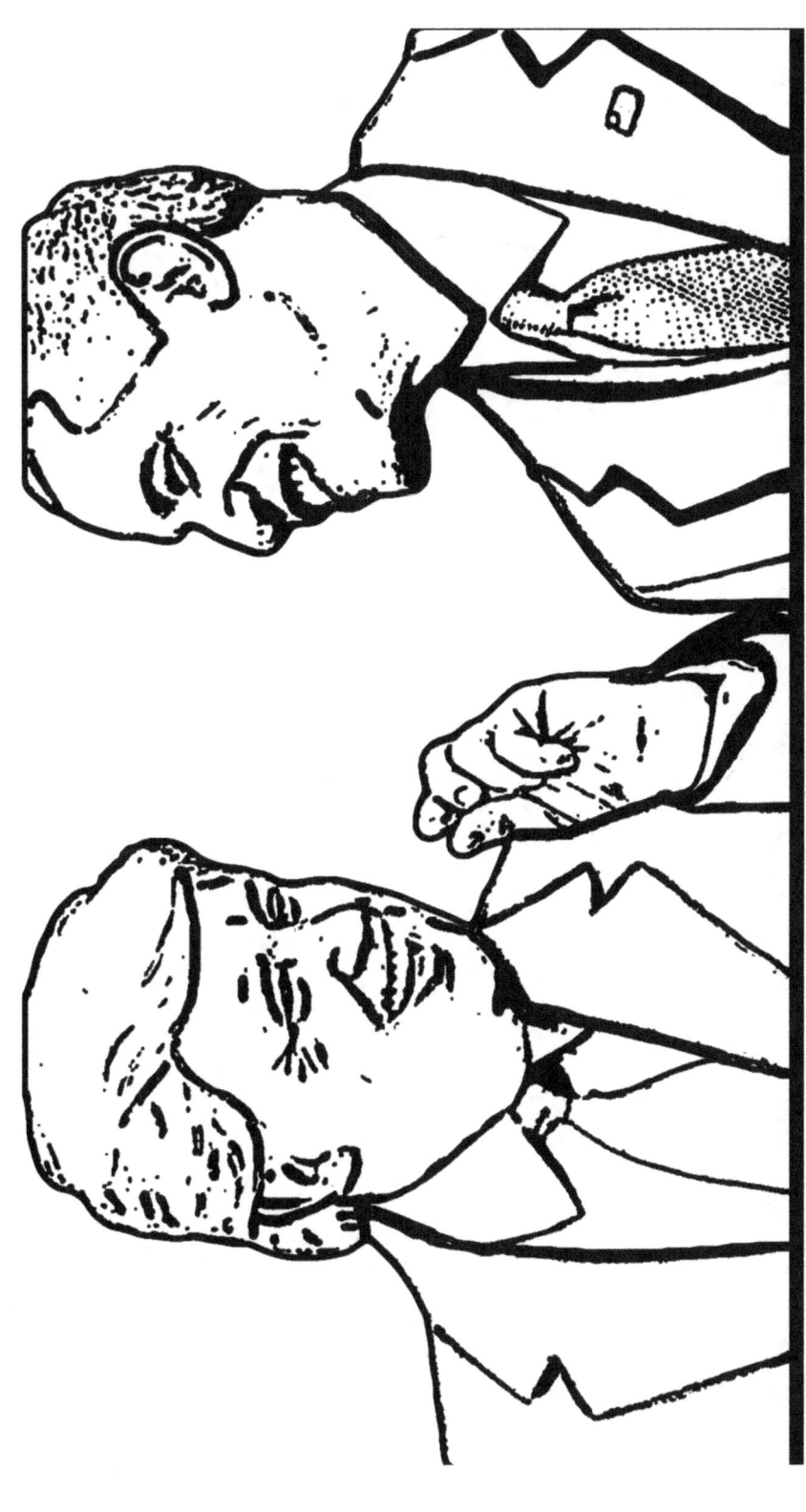

"WE GOT MORE MONEY, WE GOT MORE BRAINS, WE GOT BETTER HOUSES AND APARTMENTS, WE GOT NICER BOATS, WE'RE SMARTER THAN THEY ARE AND THEY SAY THEY'RE THE ELITE. YOU'RE THE ELITE, WE'RE THE ELITE. LET'S CALL OURSELVES, FROM NOW ON, THE SUPER ELITE."

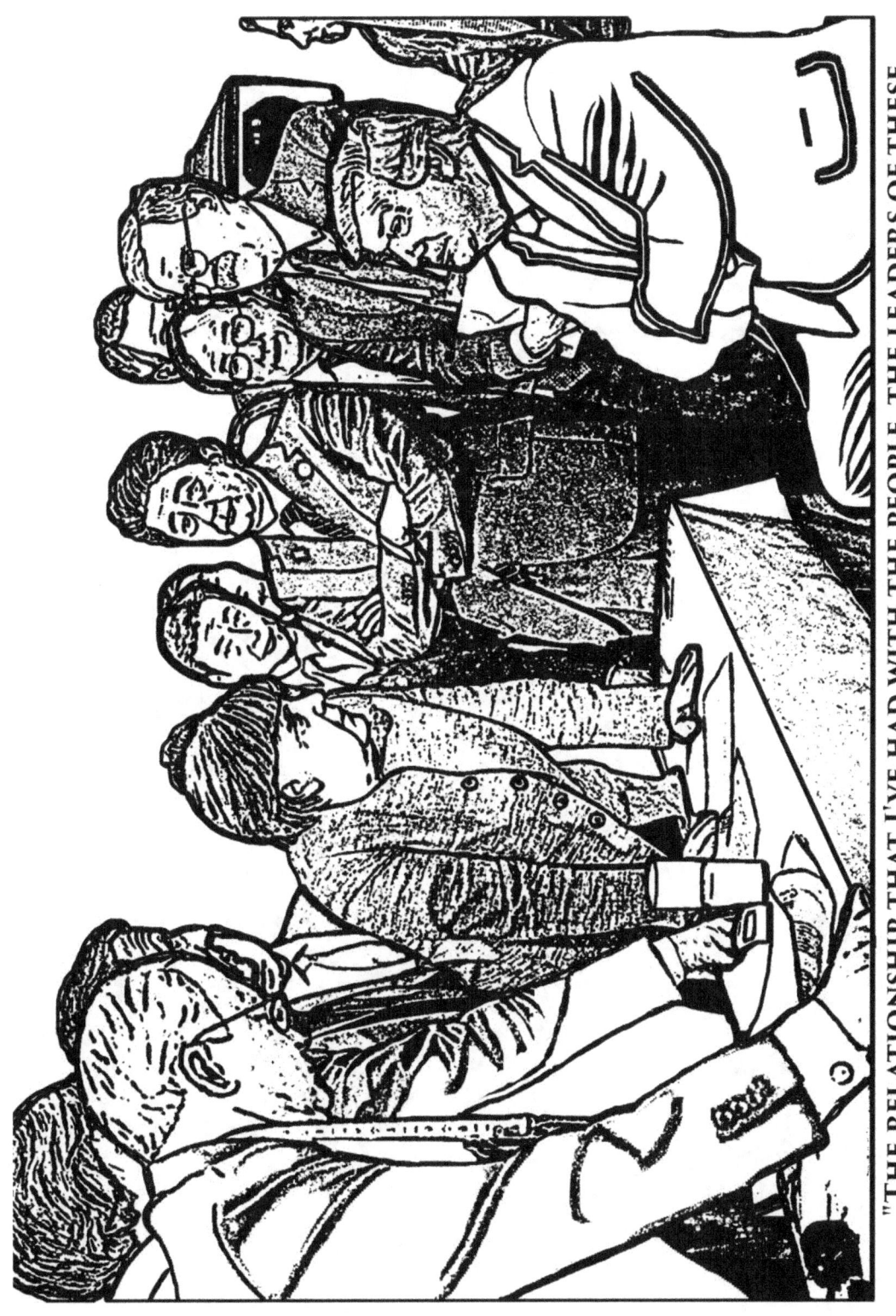

"THE RELATIONSHIP THAT I'VE HAD WITH THE PEOPLE, THE LEADERS OF THESE COUNTRIES, HAS BEEN ~ I WOULD REALLY, RATE IT ON A SCALE OF 0 TO 10, I WOULD RATE IT A 10."

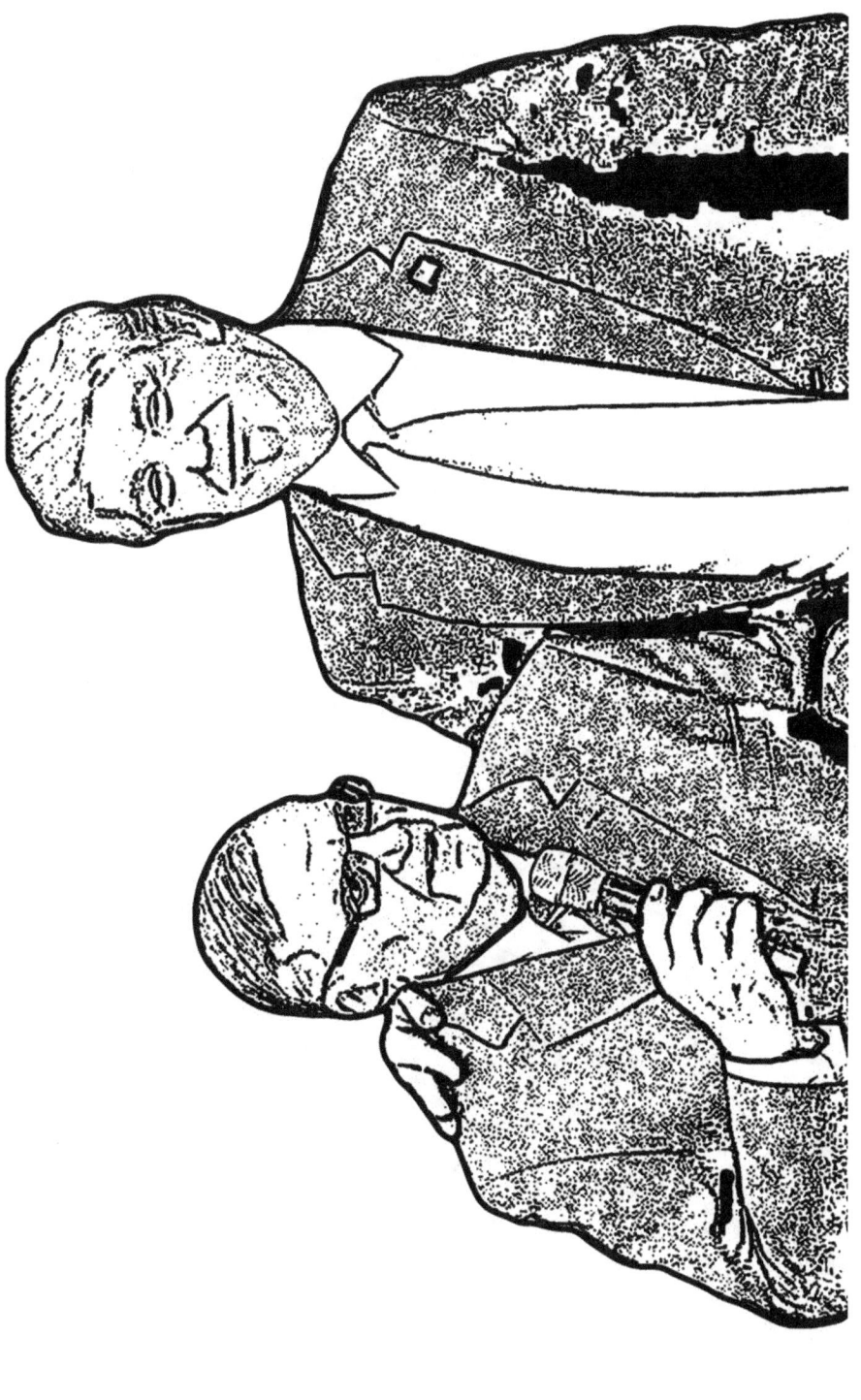

"SHERIFF JOE ARPAIO IS NOW EIGHTY-FIVE YEARS OLD, AND AFTER MORE THAN FIFTY YEARS OF ADMIRABLE SERVICE TO OUR NATION, HE IS A WORTHY CANDIDATE FOR A PRESIDENTIAL PARDON."

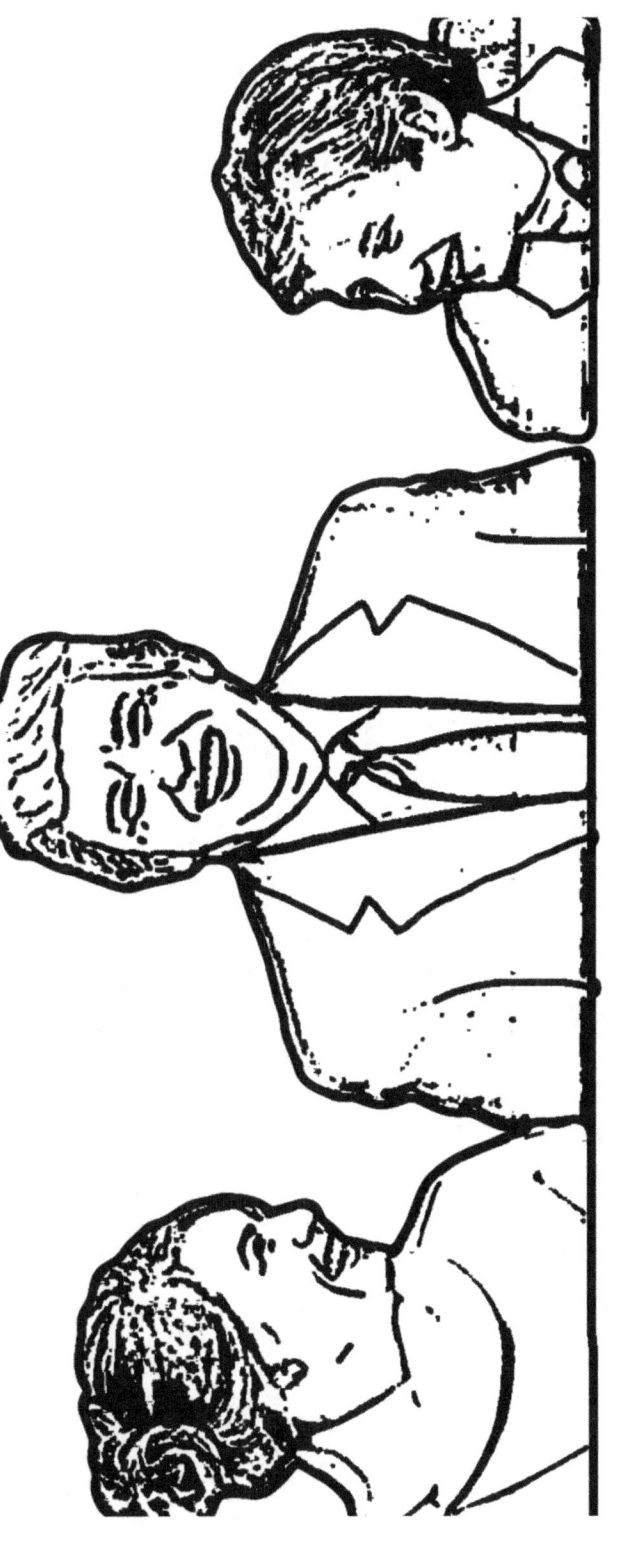

"THE POINT IS, YOU CAN NEVER BE TOO GREEDY."

Color Test Page

Color Test Page

Color Test Page